THE COMPLETE
INSTANT POT
COOKBOOK FOR UK

Surprise Your Taste Buds with 365 Days Quick,
Nutritious and Yummy Pressure Cooker Recipes and
Become A Pro in No Time

JESSE SMITH

LEGAL & DISCLAIMER

The content and information in this book is consistent and truthful, and it has been provided for informational, educational and business purposes only.
The content and information contained in this book has been compiled from reliable sources, which are accurate based on the knowledge, belief, expertise and information of the Author. The author cannot be held liable for any omissions and/or errors.

TABLE OF
CONTENT

INTRODUCTION

Innovation in kitchen technology has proven to bring miraculous results. Instant Pot pressure cookers are one great example. Closed-vessel electronic devices, which are not only energy efficient but also cook healthy and delicious food quickly, have become a must-have for every household. Instant Pot pressure cookers have garnered much recognition for their multipurpose cooking technology. There are several cooking modes available in one single appliance. It comes with various preset options, which are created to cook a meal as per the standard temperature and time without manual control. With its easy-to-use manual options, we can cook anything as per our own settings. In this Instant Pot pressure cooker cookbook, we shall discover all the flavoursome recipes which can be cooked and prepared using the Instant Pot. From routine breakfast to meaty delights and dessert treats, there is a complete range of our menu to choose your favourite meal from and cook in your Instant Pot.

CHAPTER 1 UNDERSTANDING THE INSTANT POT

Instant Pot pressure cookers are primarily divided as per their sizes, volumes, and cooking functions. It comes in several different models, whereas each model having a certain size and varying external features. As of today, there are about three unique sizes of Instant Pot available in the kitchen tech market, which includes the sizes 5 litres, 6 litres, and 8 litres. To identify a pot from its size, check out its model number. The model named IPDUO50 has a volume of 5 litres, whereas IP-DUO 60, IP LUX 60 V3, IP ULTRA, IP Smart Bluetooth, and IP-DUO plus 60, all have the size and volume of 6 litres. Lastly, IP DUO80 has a volume of about 8 litres. With the change in size, model, and capacity, the price of each device also changes. However, each model offers similar standards of features for versatile cooking. When you look for a certain model and size of Instant Pot, you must check out its dimensions and weight to match your needs.

The overall weight of all its models varies between 5-8 kg. To pick the right Pot for you, first, look for the desired size and related model, then compare the weight, dimensions, and individual prices of each Pot.

1. Base unit/ Cooking Vessel

This vessel is the primary functional unit, which contains a built-in electric heating system with special sensors for pressure and temperature control. The base is composed of a cylindrical vessel that has a stable outer body, with a visible control panel fixed on the outside of the control box. The open upper end of this vessel has handles on both sides for easy handling, a stand for the lid, and open/close marks. The heating element of the device is fixed under the base layer of this vessel. It has rims on the inside, which are used to fix the cooking pot. There are grooves on the outside to fix the condensation collector.

2. Control panel with Adjustment Keys

Every standard Instant Pot model has one prominent control panel placed in its control box. This panel contains a LED display screen; which indicates cooking mode, pressure, cooking time; errors, etc. This panel makes you select a certain for cooking through its easy-to-use button system. Its operational keys, you can set time and the desired pressure accordingly. This multifunctional Instant Pot pressure cooker has the following basic programs to allow efficient cooking:

* **Soup**
* **Rice**
* **Meat stew**
* **Multigrain**
* **Bean Chili**
* **Porridge**

* **Poultry**
* **Steam**
* **Slow Cook**
* **Yoghurt**
* **Sauté**

3. Calibrated Inner Pot

The Instant Pot cooker comes with an inner cooking pot, which is completely removable. It is made from premium quality stainless steel, which makes it dishwasher-safe and quite durable too. For good and shining clean, its outside surface is mirror polished. Whereas its bottom and underside are made from three-ply material, so the heat penetrates evenly into the food and avoid burning. The size of the inner Pot varies for each model. It is marked with grading lines from the inside.

4. Instant Pot Lid

The function of the Instant Pot lid is crucial in pressure-cooking food. The lid helps maintain both the pressure and temperature inside the vessel. For pressure cooking, this lid needs to be completely locked. The inner side of the lid contains a groove around the rim where the silicon ring is fixed. In this lid, there are two valves, the pressure valve and the float valve. The inside of the float valve is covered with an anti-block shield which prevents the valve from clogging through food particles.

* *Pressure Release handle:*

the pressure valve is controlled with the help of a pressure release handle, which is both removable and washable. To close the valve, this handle should be turned toward the "closed" sign on the lid, and to open the valve, the handle should be turned towards the "venting position." This handle can be used for "Quick release" of the steam after the cooking is finished.

* *Float Valve:*

The float valve maintains the internal pressure. When the cooker initiates "cooking" mode, the float valve is pressed downward to airtight the entire vessel. Whereas when the steam is released, the float valve comes upward back to its position.

5. Condensation or Steam Collector

The basic function of the condensation collector is to collect all the vapors and steam produced during cooking in the closed vessel. The condensation collector is fixed outside the base unit, where there are specific grooves given for the collector. After every session, this condensation collector needs to be removed and washed. Place it back into its position before the next session of cooking.

6. Accessories

The Instant Pot pressure cooker is packed with lots of other amazing accessories, which makes your cooking experience a delight. It comes with an extra glass lid to cover the food while it is slow-cooked or not cooking. There is a steel rack or steamer trivet, which is used to create multiple layers inside the cooking pot. There is also a cup, a ladle, an extra silicon ring, rice paddles, a silicon cover, and a mini mitt available with the cooker.

BENEFITS OF INSTANT POT

In a world full of advanced tech appliances, why would a person opt for Instant Pot? The sheer simplicity of its structure, the preset cooking functions, and varieties of models available, ranging both in size and functions; are a few of the features which make the Instant Pot a must-have for every kitchen. Especially for people with a busy lifestyle. The name itself indicates how time efficient the device is. However, there are many other known benefits of using an Instant Pot, and they will help you make up your mind about the device.

* *A Healthy Meal Every Time:*

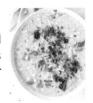

Whenever the food is cooked in a sealed vessel, it retains all of its nutrients, and the food does not lose the essential flavours and aroma. A meal cooked in Instant Pot, therefore, turns out to be healthy and nutritious. Whether you are cooking meat or vegetables, both their minerals and moisture will return to the meal without any loss.

* Time Efficient:

Instant Pot is an electronic device with a built-in heating system that effectively maintains the inner temperature of the cooking vessel and provides heat only as per the requirement. With advanced pressure-cooking technology, the food is cooked in lesser time. Sealed cooking ensures better tenderizing of meat, lentils, or beans in a few minutes.

* Energy Conservation:

Instant Pot has a controlled heat mechanism where the minimum use of electricity generates sufficient heat. Moreover, the sealed vessel ensures no heat loss into the environment. That is why Instant Pot is also energy efficient.

* Keeps the Environment Clean:

Cooking in an open pot leaves the surrounding surfaces covered in fumes and grease. The oil particles gradually settle on the surface and captivate dust over the period. Instant Pot, due to its closed lid mechanism, keeps the environment clean. Vapors released from the food are accumulated in a side chamber which can be later emptied and washed.

* Multi-Functional:

One of the greatest perks of using an Instant Pot is that it provides all functions in a single device; whether you want to pressure cook, steam the food, slow cook it, or boil it, all can be done through it. It is basically an all-in-one electric appliance that has brought more ease than ever.

HOW TO USE YOUR INSTANT POT?

Efficient functioning of the Instant Pot links directly to its operational understanding. Due to its multipurpose cooking operations, it is difficult to get away with the details of each function. Since we have already established the fact that all the functions of an Instant Pot are carried through its control panel, in this particular section, we will not only understand the use of different buttons present on this control panel, but we shall also identify all the necessary steps, required to prepare a complete meal out of an Instant Pot.

1. Open the Vessel

The appliance comes with its closed. Before and after the use, this lid should remove and closed, respectively. This lid opens with a simple rotation formula. To open the lid, you need to rotate it anticlockwise, up to 30 degrees, and reverse the same movement to lock the lid. Locking is important to seal the steam and food inside the vessel. There are arrow marks present on the lid which should be aligned with the marks on the vessel showing locked or unlocked.

2. Check All the Components

Before using the device, it is essential to check all its components, if the power cord is intact, all the valves are in their position, and the sealing ring is properly fixed, etc. If any of the components are not properly set, the device will not function well. Now that everything is set in place, you can plug in your device. Once plugged in, the LED screen of the control panel lights up.

3. Add Ingredients to the Pot

To start with the cooking, you can either remove the cooking pot from the vessel and add ingredients to it or leave it in the vessel. For meals where we start by sautéing the ingredients, the inner Pot is left inside of the vessels, and ingredients are added gradually to the Pot. The inner calibration of the Pot provides a good measurement for our food, and it also marks the limit and does not add anything above its 2/3 full limit. There must be enough space above the food so that it can easily boil or expand.

4. Sealing and Securing the Lid

For pressure cooking, the lid of the Instant Pot needs to be sealed and locked. For that, simply place the lid over the vessel and rotate it 30 degrees clockwise until it sounds clicks. There are marks on the lid: "open" and "closed," which indicate if the lid is closed. When the arrow on the vessel aligns with the close marking of the lid, it means your lid is sealed. Whenever the lid is not properly closed, the screen on the control panel flashes "Lid" to show that the lid is not in place. This is one of the security features of the Instant Pot, which does not initiate cooking without proper locking of the lid.

5. The Function of the Pressure Handle and Float Valve

For pressure cooking, both the pressure and float valves are important to deal with. The pressure valve keeps the steam locked inside the vessel, whereas the float valve maintains the amount of steam and pressure inside the appliance. The pressure valve is guarded by a pressure handle on the outside. This handle is used to close or open the pressure valve. When the tip of the handle is turned towards the 'Venting' position, it means the valve is open, and when the same handle is turned towards the 'closed' sign, it means the valve is closed. Whenever we cook food at high pressure, we need to turn the pressure valve to the closed position before initiating the operation. For other modes, where there is simple or slow cooking, keep the pressure handle in the venting position. The float valve should be pressed downward for pressure cooking; once the cooking is done and all the steam is released, then the float valve pops out back to its original position.

6. Appropriate Mode/Program

As a multipurpose Instant Pot cooker offers you several different cooking modes, each of these modes has its own preset or integrated settings to adjust both the time and pressure according to the requirement. To start the cooking process, select any of the desired programs by pressing their respective buttons or keys. Remember that each mode has its own settings; to make changes in time and pressure, use the adjustment keys. Every standard control panel of an Instant Pot pressure cooker gives you these many options:

* **Soup**	* **Steam**
* **Meat/Stew**	* **Rice**
* **Bean/Chili**	* **Multigrain**
* **Porridge**	* **Sauté**
* **Poultry**	* **Yoghurt**

Once the mode is selected, the Instant Pot will immediately switch to a Preheating State, which continues for 10 seconds. During this stage, the cooker sets its internal temperature and the internal pressure; then, it finally switches to the cooking state.

* Manual Cooking Program

To cook food at any desired time and pressure settings, use the Manual mode. It simply allows customized cooking settings. Using the button for the Manual function, you can adjust the time and pressure according to any recipe. There is, however, a limit of "240 minutes" for the cooking time. To use this option, press the manual key and then adjust the time with the timer key. Set pressure with pressure operation keys.

* Keep Warm/Cancel Key

Once the food is all cooked, the Instant Pot automatically switches to a Standby mode, where it is kept warm at low temperatures. The Warm and Cancel key allows you to either stop or cancel the operation or switch the appliance to the Warm mode. Once set, the warm mode will continue until the button is pressed again.

7. Adjusting Time and Pressure

For any cooking operation, adjustment of cooking time and pressure is vital. A slight mistake in adjusting those numbers can ruin your whole food. The keys for pressure give you to select between two to three options, LOW, Medium, and High pressure. To adjust the pressure, first press the button that says "Pressure," then the "adjust" key, and finally, either press "+" or "- "to increase or decrease the pressure, respectively.

Follow a similar pattern for time adjustment; first press the "timer' button, then the "adjustment" key. Now you can increase or decrease the number of minutes by either pressing the "+" or the "- "operation keys. Mainly the adjustment keys are there for three different types of adjustment settings:

1. To adjust and set the pressure for any selected program except for rice functions.
2. To set the temperature for Slow cook and Sauté mode.
3. To adjust the required program for "yoghurt" preparation.

CLEANING YOUR INSTANT POT PRESSURE COOKER

All electric kitchen appliance needs proper cleaning after every cooking session, especially the pressure cookers, as they have different lid and mechanism which depends on working pressure and float valve, and without a good cleaning, we can jeopardize their fine functioning. Instant Pot cannot be simply washed and cleaned like other kitchen utensils; it needs a special step-by-step cleaning procedure and extra care for cleaning. Follow the following important steps to keep your device clean and fresh as new.

1. Do not try cleaning the appliance right after the cooking. In fact, the hot device should not even be touched after every session. First, unplug the appliance, then allow it to cool for 30 minutes, then initiate cleaning.
2. The house rim inside the Instant Pot can be wiped off using a piece of cloth. Avoid washing or using water to clean this part, as it would cause bad rust over the rim.
3. First, remove the upper lid and remove the inner Pot from the vessels. Remember, this stainless-steel cooking pot is dishwasher safe, so you can directly wash it in your dishwasher. Else you can also wash it using soapy water or detergent, then rinse well under clean tap water. Before inserting it back into the vessel, make sure to let it dry completely or wipe it off using a dry piece of cloth.
4. Clean the lid by removing the pressure handle and washing this handle separately. Then uninstall the sealing ring and anti-block shield to wash them separately too. While cleaning the lid, make sure to thoroughly wash the valves to remove all the food particles stuck inside. Again, let it dry before putting it back on the device.
5. Leave the steam release pipe of the lid intact, and do not try to rub or scratch it during the cleaning. It should not be removed from the lid, so wash the lid as it is.
6. The base unit or the cooking vessel contains the entire heating element and the electrical circuit, which is why it should be kept away even from a drop of water. Avoid putting the vessel underwater, or do not immerse any part of it in the water. To clean the unit, take a dry or slightly wet piece of cloth and wipe off the outer surface. Meanwhile, make sure that the device is unplugged.
7. Do not immerse the power plug in the water. If it appears dirty, just brush off the dust from its top using a dry or slightly wet piece of cloth. Remove the plug from the socket to clean it thoroughly.
8. To clean the area underneath the device and around it, make sure to move the device and then clean the place. Do not start wiping it off by inserting the cloth underneath it.

<u>CONCLUSION</u>

This multipurpose appliance can take the place of a variety of countertop machines, including rice cookers and slow cookers, while saving lots of counter space. Who wouldn't want a pressure cooker, slow cooker, steamer, yoghurt, and rice maker all in one place? Instant Pot pressure cookers are the ultimate saviors for all the newbies who want to cook with convenience. And the recipes in this cookbook will further make it easier to create and follow a menu cooked out of an Instant Pot. So, go ahead, pick your favourites from this menu and enjoy!

CHAPTER 2 BREAKFASTS

VANILLA PANCAKE

Prep time: 5 minutes | Cook time: 50 minutes | Serves 6

INGREDIENTS:

* 3 eggs, bcatcn
* 55 g coconut flour
* 60 g heavy cream
* 25 g almond flour
* 3 tbsps. Sweetener
* 1 tsp. vanilla extract
* 1 tsp. baking powder
* Cooking spray

DIRECTIONS:

1. In a bowl, stir together the eggs, coconut flour, heavy cream, almond flour, Sweetener and vanilla extract. Whisk in the baking powder until smooth.
2. Spritz the bottom and sides of Instant Pot with cooking spray. Place the batter in the pot.
3. Set the lid in place. Select the Manual mode and set the cooking time for 50 minutes on Low Pressure. Once the timer goes off, perform a natural pressure release for 5 minutes, then release any remaining pressure. Carefully open the lid.
4. Let the pancake rest in the pot for 5 minutes before serving.

. . . .

RAISIN AND CRANBERRY COMPOTE

Prep time: 5 minutes | Cook time: 3 minutes | Makes 2½ cups

INGREDIENTS:

* 1 (340-g) package fresh or frozen cranberries
* 60 ml thawed orange juice concentrate
* 140 g packed brown sugar
* 2 tbsps. raspberry vinegar
* 70 g golden raisins
* 65 g chopped dried apricots
* 60 g chopped walnuts, toasted

DIRECTIONS:

1. Combine the cranberries, orange juice concentrate, brown sugar, and vinegar in the Instant Pot.
2. Secure the lid. Select the Manual mode and set the cooking time for 3 minutes at High Pressure.
3. Once cooking is complete, do a natural pressure release for 5 minutes, then release any remaining pressure. Carefully open the lid.
4. Stir in the raisins, apricots, and walnuts and serve warm.

. . . .

BUCKWHEAT AND STRAWBERRY PUDDING

Prep time: 5 minutes | Cook time: 7 minutes | Serves 4

INGREDIENTS:

* 170 g buckwheat groats
* 720 ml coconut milk
* 165 g chopped fresh strawberries
* 45 g unsweetened shredded coconut
* 1 tsp. cinnamon
* ½ tsp. almond extract
* ½ tsp. pure vanilla extract
* 85 g sliced almonds
* 120 ml cold coconut cream

DIRECTIONS:

1. Stir together all the ingredients, except for the almonds and coconut cream, in the Instant Pot.
2. Secure the lid. Select the Manual mode and set the cooking time for 7 minutes at High Pressure.
3. Once cooking is complete, do a natural pressure release for 20 minutes, then release any remaining pressure. Carefully open the lid.
4. Spoon the buckwheat pudding into serving dishes. Garnish with coconut cream and almonds before serving.

RAISIN AND APPLE OATMEAL

Prep time: 10 minutes | Cook time: 5 minutes | Serves 6

INGREDIENTS:

* 720 g vanilla almond milk
* 60 g oats
* 3 tbsps. brown sugar
* 110 g raisins
* 4½ tsps. butter
* ½ tsp. salt
* ¾ tsp. ground cinnamon
* 1 large apple, peeled and chopped
* 30 g chopped pecans

DIRECTIONS:

1. Combine all the ingredients except the apple and pecans in the Instant Pot.
2. Secure the lid. Select the Manual mode and set the cooking time for 5 minutes at High Pressure.
3. Once cooking is complete, do a natural pressure release for 10 minutes, then release any remaining pressure. Carefully open the lid.
4. Scatter with the chopped apple and stir well. Allow the oatmeal to sit for 1o minutes. Ladle into bowls and sprinkle the pecans on top. Serve immediately.

PEANUT BUTTER GRANOLA BARS

Prep time: 5 minutes | Cook time: 20 minutes | Serves 10

INGREDIENTS:

* 80 g quick-cooking oats
* 130 g all-natural peanut butter
* 110 g pure maple syrup
* 1 tbsp. extra-virgin olive oil
* ¼ tsp. fine sea salt
* 55 g dried cranberries or raisins
* 60 g raw pumpkin seeds
* 240 ml water

DIRECTIONS:

1. Line a 18 cm round pan with parchment paper.
2. Combine the oats, peanut butter, maple syrup, olive oil, and salt in a large bowl and stir well. Fold in the dried cranberries and pumpkin seeds, then scrape the batter into the prepared pan. Use a spatula to press the batter evenly into the bottom of the pan.
3. Pour the water into the Instant Pot and insert a trivet. Place the pan on the trivet. Cover the pan with another piece of parchment to protect the granola bars from condensation.
4. Secure the lid. Select the Manual mode and set the cooking time for 20 minutes at High Pressure.
5. Once cooking is complete, do a natural pressure release for 10 minutes, then release any remaining pressure. Carefully open the lid.
6. Remove the trivet and let the granola cool completely in the pan. Cut the cooled granola into 10 pieces and serve.

ASPARAGUS AND GRUYÈRE CHEESE FRITTATA

Prep time: 10 minutes | Cook time: 22 minutes | Serves 6

INGREDIENTS:

* 6 eggs
* 6 tbsps. heavy cream
* ½ tsp. salt
* ½ tsp. black pepper
* 1 tbsp. butter
* 70 g asparagus, chopped
* 1 clove garlic, minced
* 125 g shredded Gruyère cheese, divided
* Cooking spray
* 85 g halved cherry tomatoes
* 120 ml wate

DIRECTIONS:

1. In a large bowl, stir together the eggs, cream, salt, and pepper.
2. Set the Instant Pot on the Sauté mode and melt the butter. Add the asparagus and garlic to the pot and sauté for 2 minutes, or until the garlic is fragrant. The asparagus should still be crisp.
3. Transfer the asparagus and garlic to the bowl with the egg mixture. Stir in 100 g of the cheese. Clean the pot.
4. Spritz a baking pan with cooking spray. Spread the tomatoes in a single layer in the pan. Pour the egg mixture on top of the tomatoes and sprinkle with the remaining 25 g of the cheese. Cover the pan tightly with aluminum foil.
5. Pour the water in the Instant Pot and insert the trivet. Place the pan on the trivet.
6. Set the lid in place. Select the Manual mode and set the cooking time for 20 minutes on High Pressure. When the timer goes off, perform a quick pressure release. Carefully open the lid.
7. Remove the pan from the pot and remove the foil. Blot off any excess moisture with a paper towel. Let the frittata cool for 5 to 10 minutes before transferring onto a plate.

EGG BENEDICT

Prep time: 5 minutes | Cook time: 1 minute | Serves 3

INGREDIENTS:

* 1 tsp. butter
* 3 eggs
* ¼ tsp. salt
* ½ tsp. ground black pepper
* 240 ml water
* 3 turkey bacon slices, fried

DIRECTIONS:

1. Grease the eggs molds with the butter and crack the eggs inside. Sprinkle with salt and ground black pepper.
2. Pour the water and insert the trivet in the Instant Pot. Put the eggs molds on the trivet.
3. Set the lid in place. Select the Manual mode and set the cooking time for 1 minute on High Pressure. When the timer goes off, do a quick pressure release. Carefully open the lid.
4. Transfer the eggs onto the plate. Top the eggs with the fried bacon slices.

HAWAIIAN SWEET POTATO HASH

Prep time: 20 minutes | Cook time: 20 minutes | Serves 6

INGREDIENTS:

* 4 bacon strips, chopped
* 1 tbsp. coconut oil
* 2 large sweet potatoes, peeled and cut into 1 cm pieces
* 240 ml water
* 330 g cubed fresh pineapple
* ½ tsp. salt
* ¼ tsp. paprika
* ¼ tsp. chili powder
* ¼ tsp. pepper
* ⅛ tsp. ground cinnamon

DIRECTIONS:

1. Press the Sauté button on the Instant Pot and add the bacon. Cook for about 7 minutes, stirring occasionally, or until crisp.
2. Remove the bacon with a slotted spoon and drain on paper towels. Set aside.
3. In the Instant Pot, heat the oil until it shimmers.
4. Working in batches, add the sweet potatoes to the pot and brown each side for 3 to 4 minutes. Transfer the sweet potatoes to a large bowl and set aside.
5. Pour the water into the pot and cook for 1 minute, stirring to loosen browned bits from pan.
6. Place a steamer basket in the Instant Pot. Add the pineapple, salt, paprika, chili powder, pepper, and cinnamon to the large bowl of sweet potatoes and toss well, then transfer the mixture to the steamer basket.
7. Secure the lid. Select the Steam mode and set the cooking time for 2 minutes at High Pressure.
8. Once cooking is complete, do a quick pressure release. Carefully open the lid.
9. Top with the bacon and serve on a plate.

EGGS IN PURGATORY

Prep time: 15 minutes | Cook time: 24 minutes | Serves 4

INGREDIENTS:

* 2 (410-g) cans fire-roasted diced tomatoes, undrained
* 120 ml water
* 1 medium onion, chopped
* 2 garlic cloves, minced
* 2 tbsps. rapeseed oil
* 2 tsps. smoked paprika
* ½ tsp. crushed red pepper flakes
* ½ tsp. sugar
* 60 g tomato paste
* 4 large eggs
* 25 g shredded Monterey Jack cheese
* 2 tbsps. minced fresh parsley
* 1 (510-g) tube polenta, sliced and warmed (optional)

DIRECTIONS:

1. Place the tomatoes, water, onion, garlic, oil, paprika, red pepper flakes, and sugar into the Instant Pot and stir to combine.
2. Secure the lid. Select the Manual mode and set the cooking time for 4 minutes at High Pressure.
3. Once cooking is complete, do a quick pressure release. Carefully open the lid.
4. Set the Instant Pot to Sauté and stir in the tomato paste. Let it simmer for about 10 minutes, stirring occasionally, or until the mixture is slightly thickened.
5. With the back of a spoon, make 4 wells in the sauce and crack an egg into each. Scatter with the shredded cheese.
6. Cover (do not lock the lid) and allow to simmer for 8 to 10 minutes, or until the egg whites are completely set.
7. Sprinkle the parsley on top and serve with the polenta slices, if desired.

BACON AND EGG RISOTTO

Prep time: 12 minutes | Cook time: 12 minutes | Serves 2

INGREDIENTS:

*   360 ml chicken stock
*   2 poached eggs
*   2 tbsps. grated Parmesan cheese
*   3 chopped bacon slices
*   140 g Arborio rice

DIRECTIONS:

1. Set your Instant Pot to Sauté and add the bacon and cook for 5 minutes until crispy, stirring occasionally.
2. Carefully stir in the rice and let cook for an additional 1 minute.
3. Add the chicken stock and stir well.
4. Lock the lid. Select the Manual mode and set the cooking time for 6 minutes at Low Pressure.
5. Once cooking is complete, do a quick pressure release. Carefully open the lid.
6. Add the Parmesan cheese and keep stirring until melted. Divide the risotto between two plates. Add the eggs on the side and serve immediately.

- -

SPINACH AND HAM FRITTATA

Prep time: 3 minutes | Cook time: 10 minutes | Serves 8

INGREDIENTS:

*   135 g diced ham
*   60 g chopped spinach
*   8 eggs, beaten
*   120 ml coconut milk
*   1 onion, chopped
*   1 tsp. salt

DIRECTIONS:

1. Put all the ingredients into the Instant Pot. Stir to mix well.
2. Lock the lid. Set to Manual mode, then set the timer for 10 minutes at High Pressure.
3. Once the timer goes off, perform a natural pressure release for 5 minutes. Carefully open the lid.
4. Transfer the frittata on a plate and serve immediately.

- -

COFFEE CAKE

Prep time: 10 minutes | Cook time: 45 minutes | Serves 8

INGREDIENTS:

Cake:

*   180 g almond flour
*   25 g granulated sweetener
*   1 tsp. baking powder
*   Pinch of salt
*   2 eggs
*   120 g sour cream
*   4 tbsps. butter, melted
*   2 tsps. vanilla extract
*   2 tbsps. Sweetener
*   1½ tsps. ground cinnamon
*   Cooking spray
*   120 ml water

Icing:

*   55 g cream cheese, softened
*   25 g powdered erythritol
*   1 tbsp. heavy cream
*   ½ tsp. vanilla extract

DIRECTIONS:

1. In the bowl of a stand mixer, combine the almond flour, granulated sweetener, baking powder and salt. Mix until no lumps remain. Add the eggs, sour cream, butter and vanilla to the mixer bowl and mix until well combined.
2. In a separate bowl, mix together the Sweetener and cinnamon.
3. Spritz the baking pan with cooking spray. Pour in the cake batter and use a knife to make sure it is level around the pan. Sprinkle the cinnamon mixture on top. Cover the pan tightly with aluminum foil.
4. Pour the water and insert the trivet in the Instant Pot. Put the pan on the trivet.
5. Set the lid in place. Select the Manual mode and set the cooking time for 45 minutes on High Pressure. When the timer goes off, do a quick pressure release. Carefully open the lid.
6. Remove the cake from the pot and remove the foil. Blot off any moisture on top of the cake with a paper towel, if necessary. Let rest in the pan for 5 minutes.
7. Meanwhile, make the icing: In a small bowl, use a mixer to whip the cream cheese until it is light and fluffy. Slowly fold in the powdered erythritol and mix until well combined. Add the heavy cream and vanilla extract and mix until thoroughly combined.
8. When the cake is cooled, transfer it to a platter and drizzle the icing all over.

FRENCH EGGS

Prep time: 12 minutes | Cook time: 8 minutes | Serves 4

INGREDIENTS:

* ¼ tsp. salt
* 4 bacon slices
* 1 tbsp. olive oil
* 4 tbsps. chopped chives
* 4 eggs
* 360 ml water

DIRECTIONS:

1. Grease 4 ramekins with a drizzle of oil and crack an egg into each ramekin.
2. Add a bacon slice on top and season with salt. Sprinkle the chives on top.
3. Add 360 ml water and steamer basket to your Instant Pot. Transfer the ramekins to the basket.
4. Lock the lid. Select the Manual mode and set the cooking time for 8 minutes at High Pressure.
5. Once cooking is complete, do a quick pressure release. Carefully open the lid.
6. Serve your baked eggs immediately.

. . . .

EGGS EN COCOTTE

Prep time: 10 minutes | Cook time: 20 minutes | Serves 4

INGREDIENTS:

* 240 ml water
* 1 tbsp. butter
* 4 tbsps. heavy whipping cream
* 4 eggs
* 1 tbsp. chives
* Salt and pepper, to taste

DIRECTIONS:

1. Arrange a steamer rack in the Instant Pot, then pour in the water.
2. Grease four ramekins with butter.
3. Divide the heavy whipping cream in the ramekins, then break each egg in each ramekin.
4. Sprinkle them with chives, salt, and pepper.
5. Arrange the ramekins on the steamer rack.
6. Lock the lid. Set to the Manual mode, then set the timer for 20 minutes at High Pressure.
7. Once the timer goes off, perform a natural pressure release for 10 minutes, then release any remaining pressure. Carefully open the lid.
8. Transfer them on a plate and serve immediately.

. . . .

QUINOA AND TOMATO CREAM BOWL

Prep time: 12 minutes | Cook time: 12 minutes | Serves 6

INGREDIENTS:

* 1 tbsp. grated ginger
* 1 (700 g) can tomatoes, chopped
* 40 g quinoa
* 350 g coconut milk
* 1 small yellow onion, chopped

DIRECTIONS:

1. In the Instant Pot, mix the onion with quinoa, tomatoes, milk and ginger, and stir well.
2. Lock the lid. Select the Manual mode and cook for 12 minutes at High Pressure.
3. Once cooking is complete, do a natural pressure release for 5 minutes, then release any remaining pressure. Carefully open the lid.
4. Stir the mixture one more time and divide into bowls to serve.

CHAPTER 3 GRAIN AND RICE

FETA AND RED ONION COUSCOUS PILAF

Prep time: 5 minutes | Cook time: 5 minutes | Serves 4

INGREDIENTS:

* 2 tbsps. vegetable oil
* 1 tsp. cumin seeds
* 1 tsp. ground turmeric
* 120 g frozen peas and carrots
* 175 g couscous
* 80 g diced yellow onion
* 1 tsp. salt
* 1 tsp. garam masala
* 240 ml water
* 80 g chopped red onion
* 120 g crumbled feta cheese
* Black pepper, to taste

DIRECTIONS:

1. Press the Sauté button on the Instant Pot and heat the oil.
2. Once the oil is hot, stir in the cumin seeds and turmeric, allowing them to sizzle for 10 seconds. Turn off the Instant Pot.
3. Add the peas and carrots, couscous, yellow onion, salt, garam masala, and water. Stir to combine.
4. Lock the lid. Select the Manual mode and set the cooking time for 3 minutes at High Pressure.
5. When the timer beeps, perform a natural pressure release for 5 minutes, then release any remaining pressure. Carefully remove the lid.
6. Stir in the red onion and feta cheese. Season to taste with black pepper and serve.

. . . .

CRANBERRY AND ALMOND QUINOA PILAF

Prep time: 2 minutes | Cook time: 10 minutes | Serves 2 to 4

INGREDIENTS:

* 180 g quinoa, rinsed
* 480 ml water
* 110 g dried cranberries
* 55 g slivered almonds
* 65 g salted sunflower seeds

DIRECTIONS:

1. Combine the water and quinoa in the Instant Pot.
2. Lock the lid. Select the Manual mode and set the cooking time for 10 minutes at High Pressure.
3. Once cooking is complete, do a quick pressure release. Carefully open the lid.
4. Add the cranberries, almonds, and sunflower seeds and gently mix until well incorporated. Serve warm.

. . . .

QUINOA RISOTTO

Prep time: 6 minutes | Cook time: 3 hours | Serves 4

INGREDIENTS:

* 120 g diced onion
* 1 garlic clove, minced
* 1 tbsp. butter
* Salt and pepper, to taste
* 600 ml chicken stock
* 180 g rinsed quinoa
* 25 g shredded Parmesan cheese

DIRECTIONS:

1. Combine the onion, garlic, and butter in a microwave-safe bowl.
2. Microwave for 5 minutes, stirring every 90 seconds.
3. Put the mixture in the Instant Pot.
4. Add the salt, pepper, stock, and quinoa and stir to combine.
5. Lock the lid. Select the Slow Cook mode, then set the timer for 3 hours at High Pressure.
6. Once the timer goes off, perform a natural release for 10 minutes, then release any remaining pressure. Carefully open the lid.
7. Mix the Parmesan into the mixture. Taste and adjust the seasoning, if needed.

QUINOA WITH SPINACH

Prep time: 5 minutes | Cook time: 2 minutes | Serves 4

INGREDIENTS:

* 270 g quinoa, rinsed
* 360 ml water
* 120 g spinach
* 1 pepper, chopped
* 3 stalks of celery, chopped
* ¼ tsp. salt

DIRECTIONS:

1. Combine all the ingredients in the Instant Pot.
2. Secure the lid. Select the Manual mode and set the cooking time for 2 minutes at High Pressure.
3. Once cooking is complete, do a natural pressure release for 10 minutes, then release any remaining pressure. Carefully open the lid.
4. Fluff the quinoa and serve.

. . . .

PARMESAN RISOTTO

Prep time: 6 minutes | Cook time: 20 minutes | Serves 4

INGREDIENTS:

* 960 ml chicken stock, divided
* 4 tbsps. butter
* 1 small onion, diced
* 2 garlic cloves, minced
* 300 g Arborio rice
* Salt and pepper, to taste
* 25 g shredded Parmesan cheese

DIRECTIONS:

1. Set the Instant Pot to sauté and melt the butter.
2. Mix the onions in and let them cook for 2 minutes until they have become soft.
3. Add the garlic and rice and stir. Cook for 1 more minute.
4. Add 240 ml of stock and cook about 3 minutes, or until the stock is absorbed.
5. Add 720 ml of stock, salt, and pepper.
6. Sprinkle with Parmesan cheese.
7. Lock the lid. Select the Manual mode, then set the timer for 10 minutes at Low Pressure.
8. Once the timer goes off, perform a natural release for 5 minutes, then release any remaining pressure. Carefully open the lid.
9. Ladle the rice into bowls and serve.

. . . .

BLACK-EYED BEAN RICE BOWL

Prep time: 15 minutes | Cook time: 14 minutes | Serves 4

INGREDIENTS:

* 1 tsp. extra-virgin olive oil
* 1 large onion, diced
* 2 carrots, diced
* 3 celery stalks, diced
* 3 cloves garlic, minced
* 240 g dried Black-eyed beans
* 100 g white rice
* 1 medium tomato, diced
* 1 tsp. dried oregano
* 1 tsp. dried parsley
* ¼ tsp. ground cumin
* 1 tsp. crushed red pepper
* ¼ tsp. ground black pepper
* 55 g tomato paste
* 600 ml vegetable stock
* 2 tbsps. lemon juice
* Salt, to taste

DIRECTIONS:

1. Select the Sauté setting of the Instant Pot and heat the oil until shimmering.
2. Add the onion, carrots, celery and garlic and sauté for 6 minutes or until tender.
3. Add the Black-eyed beans, rice, tomato, oregano, parsley, cumin red and black peppers, tomato paste and stock to the onion mixture and stir to combine.
4. Put the lid on. Select the Manual setting and set the timer for 8 minutes at High Pressure.
5. When timer beeps, let the pressure release naturally for 5 minutes, then release any remaining pressure. Open the lid.
6. Mix in the lemon juice and salt before serving.

ARTICHOKE CORN RISOTTO

Prep time: 15 minutes | Cook time: 13 minutes | Serves 4

INGREDIENTS:

* 2 tbsps. olive oil
* 2 large white onions, chopped
* 1 medium courgette, chopped
* 4 garlic cloves, minced
* Salt and black pepper, to taste
* 200 g Arborio rice
* 120 ml white wine
* 600 ml chicken stock
* 290 g corn kernels
* 1 (170-g) can artichokes, drained and chopped
* 100 g grated Parmesan cheese
* 3 tbsps. lemon juice
* 1 tbsp. lemon zest
* 10 g chopped basil, plus more for garnish

DIRECTIONS:

1. Set the Instant Pot on the Sauté function and heat the olive oil. Add the onions, courgette and garlic to the pot and sauté for 5 minutes, or until tender. Season with salt and pepper. Stir in the rice and cook for 2 minutes, or until translucent.
2. Pour in the white wine and keep cooking until it has a thick consistency and reduces about one-third. Stir in the chicken stock, corn, salt and pepper.
3. Lock the lid. Select the Manual mode and set the cooking time for 6 minutes at High Pressure. When the timer goes off, use a natural pressure release for 15 minutes, then release any remaining pressure. Carefully open the lid.
4. Add the artichokes, cheese, lemon juice and zest and whisk until risotto is sticky. Stir in the chopped basil and transfer the risotto into bowls. Serve garnished with the basil.

MINT AND PEA RISOTTO

Prep time: 5 minutes | Cook time: 20 minutes | Serves 2

INGREDIENTS:

* 2 tbsps. coconut oil
* 1 onion, peeled and diced
* ½ tsp. garlic powder
* 100 g barley
* 240 ml vegetable stock, divided
* Salt and pepper, to taste
* 60 g fresh peas
* ¼ tsp. lime zest
* 10 g chopped fresh mint leaves

DIRECTIONS:

1. Press the Sauté button on the Instant Pot and heat the oil.
2. Add the onion and stir-fry for 5 minutes.
3. Add garlic powder and barley and cook for 1 minute more.
4. Pour in 120 ml of vegetable stock and stir for 3 minutes until it is absorbed by barley.
5. Add the remaining 120 ml of stock, salt, and pepper.
6. Secure the lid. Select the Manual mode and set the cooking time for 10 minutes at High Pressure.
7. Once cooking is complete, do a natural pressure release for 10 minutes, then release any remaining pressure. Carefully open the lid.
8. Stir in peas, lime zest, and mint and let sit for 3 minutes until heated through. Serve immediately.

MUSHROOM BARLEY RISOTTO

Prep time: 10 minutes | Cook time: 40 minutes | Serves 6

INGREDIENTS:

* 3 tbsps. butter
* 1 onion, finely chopped
* 100 g coarsely chopped shiitake mushrooms
* 100 g coarsely chopped cremini mushrooms
* 100 g coarsely chopped brown bella mushrooms
* 1 tsp. salt
* 1 tsp. freshly ground black pepper
* 1 tsp. Italian dried herb seasoning
* 200 g pearl barley
* 1 (910-g) container vegetable stock
* 50 g shredded Parmesan cheese

DIRECTIONS:

1. Set your Instant Pot to Sauté and melt the butter.
2. Add the onion and cook for about 3 minutes, or until the onion is translucent. Mix in the mushrooms, salt, pepper, and Italian seasoning. Cook for 5 to 6 minutes or until the mushrooms shrink. Stir in the barley and stock.
3. Secure the lid. Select the Manual mode and set the cooking time for 30 minutes at High Pressure.
4. Once cooking is complete, do a natural pressure release for 10 minutes, then release any remaining pressure. Carefully open the lid.
5. Stir in the Parmesan cheese. Serve hot.

FARRO RISOTTO WITH MUSHROOM

Prep time: 10 minutes | Cook time: 30 minutes | Serves 3

INGREDIENTS:

* 00 g farro
* 2 tbsps. barley
* 300 g chopped mushrooms
* 1 tbsp. red curry paste
* 1 jalapeño pepper, seeded and chopped
* 1 tbsp. shallot powder
* 2 tbsps. onion powder
* Salt and pepper, to taste
* 4 garlic cloves, minced
* 360 ml water
* 2 tomatoes, diced
* Chopped coriander, for serving
* Chopped spring onions, for serving

DIRECTIONS:

1. Combine all the ingredients, except for the tomatoes, coriander, and spring onion, in the Instant Pot.
2. Secure the lid. Select the Manual mode and set the cooking time for 30 minutes at High Pressure.
3. Once cooking is complete, do a quick pressure release. Carefully open the lid.
4. Stir in the tomatoes and let sit for 2 to 3 minutes until warmed through. Sprinkle with the coriander and spring onions and serve.

· ·

SPICY CHICKEN BULGUR

Prep time: 10 minutes | Cook time: 19 to 20 minutes | Serves 2

INGREDIENTS:

* ½ tbsp. sesame oil
* 230 g chicken breasts, boneless and skinless, cut into bite-sized pieces
* ½ onion, chopped
* 1 tsp. minced fresh garlic
* 2.5 cm ginger, peeled and sliced
* 1 Bird's-eye chili pepper, deseeded and minced
* 240 ml chicken stock
* 120 ml coconut milk
* 100 g bulgur
* 1 tsp. garam masala
* ½ tsp. turmeric powder
* ½ tsp. ground cumin
* Sea salt and ground black pepper, to taste
* 1 tbsp. chopped fresh coriander

DIRECTIONS:

1. Set the Instant Pot to the Sauté mode and heat the sesame oil. Add the chicken breasts to the pot and sear for 3 to 4 minutes, or until lightly browned. Transfer to a plate and set aside.
2. Add the onion to the pot and sauté for 5 minutes, or until just softened and fragrant. Stir in the garlic and continue to sauté for 1 minute.
3. Return the cooked chicken breasts to the pot and stir in the remaining ingredients, except for the coriander.
4. Set the lid in place. Select the Manual setting and set the cooking time for 10 minutes on High Pressure. When the timer goes off, perform a natural pressure release for 10 minutes, then release any remaining pressure. Open the lid.
5. Transfer the chicken mixture to bowls and serve topped with fresh coriander

· ·

PRAWNS AND BROCCOLI QUINOA BOWL

Prep time: 10 minutes | Cook time: 11 minutes | Serves 4

INGREDIENTS:

* 2 tbsps. butter
* 1 red pepper, chopped
* 1 medium white onion, finely diced
* 4 garlic cloves, minced
* 2 tsps. smoked paprika
* 270 g quick-cooking quinoa
* 720 ml chicken stock
* Salt and black pepper, to taste
* 455 g jumbo prawns, peeled and deveined
* 180 g broccoli florets
* 1 lemon, zested and juiced
* 3 spring onions, chopped

DIRECTIONS:

1. Set the Instant Pot to the Sauté mode and melt the butter. Add the pepper and onion to the pot and sauté for 4 minutes. Add the garlic and paprika, and sauté for 1 minute. Stir in the quinoa, chicken stock, salt and pepper.
2. Lock the lid. Select the Manual mode and set the cooking time for 1 minute on High Pressure. Once cooking is complete, use a quick pressure release. Carefully open the lid.
3. Add the prawns, broccoli, lemon zest and juice to the pot. Select the Sauté mode and cook for 5 minutes, or until prawns are pink.
4. Garnish with the chopped spring onions and serve.

MUSHROOM POLENTA

Prep time: 5 minutes | Cook time: 23 minutes | Serves 4

INGREDIENTS:

* 160 g polenta
* 960 ml vegetable stock
* 1 tbsp. butter
* 2 portobello mushrooms caps, finely chopped
* 1 tsp. onion powder
* 1 tsp. salt
* 1 tsp. freshly ground black peppe

DIRECTIONS:

1. In a large bowl, whisk together the polenta and stock until there are no lumps. Set aside.
2. Set your Instant Pot to Sauté and melt the butter.
3. Add the mushrooms, onion powder, salt, and pepper, and sauté for 2 minutes. Add the polenta mix to the Instant Pot, stirring well.
4. Lock the lid. Select the Porridge mode and set the cooking time for 20 minutes at High Pressure.
5. When the timer beeps, perform a natural pressure release for 10 minutes, then release any remaining pressure. Carefully remove the lid.
6. Stir the polenta and serve hot.

. . . .

PEARL BARLEY WITH PEPPERS

Prep time: 5 minutes | Cook time: 25 minutes | Serves 2

INGREDIENTS:

* 1 tbsp. sesame oil
* ½ yellow onion, chopped
* 1 garlic clove, minced1 pepper, deseeded and chopped
* 1 jalapeño pepper, deseeded and chopped
* 360 ml vegetable stock
* 150 g pearl barley, rinsed
* 2 tbsps. chopped chives

DIRECTIONS:

1. Set the Instant Pot to the Sauté mode and heat the oil. Add the onion to the pot and sauté for 3 minutes, or until just tender and fragrant. Add the garlic, pepper and jalapeño pepper to the pot and sauté for 2 minutes, or until fragrant. Stir in the vegetable stock and pearl barley.
2. Lock the lid. Select the Multigrain mode and set the cooking time for 20 minutes on High Pressure. When the timer goes off, perform a quick pressure release. Carefully open the lid.
3. Fluff the pearl barley mixture with a fork. Serve garnished with the chopped chives.

. . . .

SPINACH AND TOMATO COUSCOUS

Prep time: 10 minutes | Cook time: 8 minutes | Serves 4

INGREDIENTS:

* 2 tbsps. butter
* 175 g couscous
* 300 ml water
* 15 g chopped spinach
* 1½ tomatoes, chopped

DIRECTIONS:

1. Set your Instant Pot to Sauté and melt the butter.
2. Add the couscous and cook for 1 minute.
3. Pour in the water and stir well.
4. Lock the lid. Select the Manual mode and set the cooking time for 5 minutes at High Pressure.
5. When the timer beeps, perform a quick pressure release. Carefully remove the lid.
6. Transfer the couscous to a large bowl. Add the spinach and tomatoes, stir, and serve.

CHAPTER 4 NOODLES AND PASTA

DUO-CHEESE MUSHROOM PASTA

Prep time: 10 minutes | Cook time: 5 minutes | Serves 4

INGREDIENTS:

* 2 tbsps. butter
* 3 cloves garlic, minced
* 1 tsp. dried thyme
* ½ tsp. red pepper flakes
* 230 g cremini mushrooms, trimmed and sliced
* 160 g chopped onion
* 420 ml water
* 1 tsp. salt
* 1 tsp. black pepper
* 230 g fettuccine, broken in half
* 230 g Mascarpone cheese
* 100 g shredded Parmesan cheese
* 2 tsps. fresh thyme leaves, for garnish

DIRECTIONS:

1. Press the Sauté button on the Instant Pot and melt the butter. Add the garlic, thyme, and red pepper flakes to the pot and sauté for 30 seconds. Stir in the mushrooms, onion, water, salt and pepper.
2. Add the fettuccine, pushing it down into the liquid. Add the Mascarpone on top of the pasta. Do not stir.
3. Lock the lid. Select the Manual mode and set the cooking time for 5 minutes on High Pressure. Once the timer goes off, perform a natural pressure release for 5 minutes, then release any remaining pressure. Carefully open the lid.
4. Stir in the Parmesan cheese.
5. Divide the pasta among four dishes, garnish with the thyme and serve.

SPINACH AND PINE NUT FUSILLI PASTA

Prep time: 5 minutes | Cook time: 12 minutes | Serves 4

INGREDIENTS:

* 1 tbsp. butter
* 2 garlic cloves, crushed
* 455 g spinach
* 455 g fusilli pasta
* Salt and black pepper, to taste
* Water, as needed
* 2 garlic cloves, chopped
* 35 g chopped pine nuts
* Grated cheese, for serving

DIRECTIONS:

1. Press the Sauté button on the Instant Pot and melt the butter. Add the crushed garlic and spinach to the pot and sauté for 6 minutes. Add the pasta, salt and pepper. Pour in the water to cover the pasta and mix.
2. Set the lid in place. Select the Manual mode and set the cooking time for 6 minutes on Low Pressure. When the timer goes off, do a quick pressure release. Carefully open the lid.
3. Stir in the chopped garlic and nuts. Garnish with the cheese and serve.

MUSTARD MACARONI AND CHEESE

Prep time: 10 minutes | Cook time: 6 minutes | Serves 4 to 6

INGREDIENTS:

* 455 g elbow macaroni
* 960 ml chicken stock or vegetable stock, low sodium
* 3 tbsps. unsalted butter
* 120 g sour cream
* 340 g shredded Cheddar cheese
* 50 g shredded Parmesan cheese
* 1½ tsps. yellow mustard
* ⅛ tsp. cayenne pepper

DIRECTIONS:

1. Add the macaroni, stock, and butter to your Instant Pot.
2. Secure the lid. Press the Manual button on the Instant Pot and set the cooking time for 6 minutes on High Pressure.
3. Once cooking is complete, perform a quick pressure release. Carefully remove the lid.
4. Stir in the sour cream, cheese, mustard, and cayenne pepper.
5. Let stand for 5 minutes. Stir well.
6. Serve immediately.

SPINACH AND MUSHROOM PASTA

Prep time: 5 minutes | Cook time: 10 minutes | Serves 4

INGREDIENTS:

* 1 tbsp. oil
* 230 g mushrooms, minced
* ½ tsp. salt
* ½ tsp. black ground pepper
* 230 g uncooked spaghetti pasta
* 420 ml water
* 140 g spinach
* 115 g pesto
* 35 g grated Parmesan cheese

DIRECTIONS:

1. Press the Sauté button on the Instant Pot and heat the oil. Add the mushrooms, salt and pepper to the pot and sauté for 5 minutes. Add the pasta and water.
2. Set the lid in place. Select the Manual mode and set the cooking time for 5 minutes on High Pressure. When the timer goes off, do a quick pressure release. Carefully open the lid.
3. Stir in the spinach, pesto, and cheese. Serve immediately.

. . . .

CHERRY TOMATO FARFALLE WITH PESTO

Prep time: 5 minutes | Cook time: 8 to 9 minutes | Serves 2 to 4

INGREDIENTS:

* 120 g farfalle
* 960 ml water
* 175 g vegan pesto sauce
* 150 g cherry tomatoes, quartered

DIRECTIONS:

1. Place the farfalle and water in your Instant Pot.
2. Secure the lid. Press the Manual button and cook for 7 minutes at High Pressure.
3. Once cooking is complete, do a quick pressure release. Carefully remove the lid.
4. Drain the pasta and transfer it back to the pot.
5. Stir in the sauce.
6. Press the Sauté button on your Instant Pot and cook for 1 to 2 minutes.
7. Fold in the tomatoes and stir to combine.
8. Transfer to a serving dish and serve immediately.

. . . .

SPINACH LEMON PASTA

Prep time: 5 minutes | Cook time: 4 minutes | Serves 6

INGREDIENTS:

* 455 g fusilli pasta
* 120 g chopped fresh spinach
* 960 ml vegetable stock
* 2 cloves garlic, crushed and minced
* 240 ml plain coconut milk
* 1 tsp. lemon zest
* 1 tsp. lemon juice
* 10 g chopped fresh parsley
* 1 tbsp. chopped fresh mint
* ½ tsp. sea salt
* ½ tsp. coarse ground black pepper

DIRECTIONS:

1. Stir together the fusilli pasta, spinach, vegetable stock and garlic in the Instant Pot.
2. Set the lid in place. Select the Manual mode and set the cooking time for 4 minutes on High Pressure.
3. Meanwhile, whisk together the coconut milk, lemon zest and lemon juice in a bowl.
4. When the timer goes off, do a quick pressure release. Carefully open the lid. Drain off any excess liquid that might remain.
5. Add the coconut milk mixture to the pasta, along with the parsley and mint. Season with salt and pepper.
6. Stir gently and let sit for 5 minutes before serving.

BEEF MINCE PASTA

Prep time: 5 minutes | Cook time: 11 to 13 minutes | Serves 4

INGREDIENTS:

* 1 tsp. olive oil
* 455 g beef mince
* 230 g dried pasta
* 680 g pasta sauce
* 1120 ml water
* Salt and ground black pepper, to taste
* Italian seasoning, to taste

DIRECTIONS:

1. Press the Sauté button on the Instant Pot. Add the oil and let heat for 1 minute.
2. Fold in the beef mince and cook for 3 to 5 minutes until browned, stirring frequently.
3. Mix in the pasta, sauce and water and stir to combine.
4. Secure the lid. Press the Manual button on the Instant Pot and set the cooking time for 7 minutes on High Pressure.
5. Once cooking is complete, do a quick pressure release. Carefully remove the lid.
6. Stir in salt, pepper, and Italian seasoning and stir well.
7. Transfer to a serving dish and serve immediately.

. . . .

CAPER AND OLIVE PASTA

Prep time: 10 minutes | Cook time: 5 minutes | Serves 4

INGREDIENTS:

* 3 cloves garlic, minced
* 380 g of pasta such as penne or fusilli (short pasta)
* 960 ml of pasta sauce (homemade or store-bought)
* 720 ml of water, plus more as needed
* 1 tbsp. of capers
* 70 g of Kalamata olives, sliced
* ¼ teaspoon. of crushed red pepper flakes
* Salt and pepper, to taste

DIRECTIONS:

1. Press the Sauté button on your Instant Pot and add the garlic.
2. Add a splash of water and cook for about 30 seconds until fragrant.
3. Mix in the pasta, pasta sauce, water, capers, olives, and crushed red pepper flakes and stir to combine.
4. Lock the lid. Press the Manual button on the Instant Pot and set the cooking time for 5 minutes on High Pressure.
5. Once the timer goes off, use a quick pressure release. Carefully remove the lid.
6. Fold in the pasta and sprinkle with salt and pepper. Stir well.
7. Serve immediately.

. . . .

PASTA CARBONARA

Prep time: 10 minutes | Cook time: 8 to 9 minutes | Serves 4

INGREDIENTS:

* 455 g pasta dry such as rigatoni, penne
* 960 ml water
* ¼ tsp. salt
* 4 large eggs
* 100 g grated Parmesan cheese
* Ground black pepper, to taste
* 230 g bacon pancetta
* 4 tbsps. heavy cream

DIRECTIONS:

1. Place the pasta, water, and salt in your Instant Pot.
2. Secure the lid. Press the Manual button and cook for 5 minutes at High Pressure.
3. Meantime, beat together the eggs, cheese and black pepper in a mixing bowl until well mixed.
4. Cook the bacon on medium heat in a frying pan for 3 minutes until crispy.
5. Once cooking is complete, do a quick pressure release. Carefully remove the lid.
6. Select the Sauté mode. Transfer the bacon to the pot and cook for 30 seconds.
7. Stir in the egg mixture and heavy cream.
8. Secure the lid and let stand for 5 minutes.
9. Transfer to a serving dish and serve.

BOW TIE PASTA

Prep time: 5 minutes | Cook time: 11 to 12 minutes | Serves 4 to 5

INGREDIENTS:

* 1 Vidalia onion, diced
* 2 garlic cloves, minced
* 1 tbsp. olive oil
* 840 ml water
* 285 g bow tie pasta
* Grated zest and juice of 1 lemon
* 35 g black olives, pitted and chopped
* Salt and freshly ground black pepper, to taste

DIRECTIONS:

1. Press the Sauté button on the Instant Pot and heat the oil. Add the onion and garlic to the pot. Cook for 7 to 8 minutes, stirring occasionally, or until the onion is lightly browned.
2. Add the water and pasta.
3. Set the lid in place. Select the Manual mode and set the cooking time for 4 minutes on High Pressure. When the timer goes off, do a quick pressure release. Carefully open the lid.
4. Stir the pasta and drain any excess water. Stir in the lemon zest and juice and the olives. Season with salt and pepper.
5. Serve immediately.

....

SEAFOOD PASTA WITH TOMATOES

Prep time: 15 minutes | Cook time: 14 minutes | Serves 4 to 6

INGREDIENTS:

* 1 tbsp. olive oil
* 2 cloves garlic, chopped
* 1 medium onion, chopped
* 1 red pepper, chopped
* 2 tomatoes, chopped
* 120 ml dry white wine
* 190 g macaroni
* 480 ml vegetable stock
* 310 g frozen mixed seafood
* 1 tbsp. tomato purée
* 1 tsp. mixed herbs
* ½ tsp. salt
* ½ tsp. ground black pepper
* 50 g grated Parmesan cheese

DIRECTIONS:

1. Press the Sauté button on your Instant Pot. Add and heat the oil.
2. Add the garlic and onion and cook for 2 minutes, stirring occasionally.
3. Fold in the pepper and tomatoes and cook for an additional 2 minutes.
4. Add the wine and stir well. Let simmer for 5 minutes.
5. Add the macaroni, stock, seafood, tomato purée, and herbs. Sprinkle with salt and pepper. Stir until well mixed.
6. Select the Manual mode and cook for 5 minutes on High Pressure.
7. Once the timer goes off, perform a quick pressure release. Carefully remove the lid.
8. Serve topped with the cheese.

....

COURGETTE PENNE PASTA

Prep time: 10 minutes | Cook time: 10 minutes | Serves 5

INGREDIENTS:

* 1 tbsp. butter
* 1 yellow onion, thinly sliced
* 1 shallot, finely chopped
* Salt and black pepper, to taste
* 2 garlic cloves, minced
* 12 mushrooms, thinly sliced
* 1 courgette, thinly sliced
* Pinch of dried oregano
* Pinch of dried basil
* 480 ml water
* 240 ml vegetable stock
* 2 tbsps. soy sauce
* Splash of sherry wine
* 425 g penne pasta
* 145 g tomato paste

DIRECTIONS:

1. Press the Sauté button on the Instant Pot and melt the butter. Add the onion, shallot, salt and pepper to the pot and sauté for 3 minutes. Add the garlic and continue to sauté for 1 minute.
2. Stir in the mushrooms, courgette, oregano and basil. Cook for 1 minute more. Pour in the water, stock, soy sauce and wine. Add the penne, tomato paste, salt and pepper.
3. Set the lid in place. Select the Manual mode and set the cooking time for 5 minutes on High Pressure. When the timer goes off, do a quick pressure release. Carefully open the lid.
4. Serve hot.

PENNE PASTA WITH TOMATO-VODKA SAUCE

Prep time: 5 minutes | Cook time: 4 minutes | Serves 2

INGREDIENTS:

* 55 g uncooked penne pasta
* 75 g crushed tomatoes
* 240 ml water
* 30 ml coconut oil
* 1 tbsp. vodka
* 1 tsp. garlic powder
* ½ tsp. salt
* ¼ tsp. paprika
* 120 ml coconut cream
* 5 g minced coriander

DIRECTIONS:

1. Add all the ingredients, except for the coconut cream and coriander, to the Instant Pot and stir to combine.
2. Set the lid in place. Select the Manual mode and set the cooking time for 4 minutes on High Pressure. When the timer goes off, do a quick pressure release. Carefully open the lid.
3. Stir in the coconut cream and fresh coriander and serve hot.

. . . .

TUNA NOODLE CASSEROLE WITH CHEESE

Prep time: 10 minutes | Cook time: 3 minutes | Serves 6

INGREDIENTS:

* 340 g egg noodles
* 1 (230- to 340-g) can tuna albacore chunk preferred, drained
* 120 g frozen peas
* 100 g mushrooms, sliced
* 720 ml chicken stock
* 1 tsp. salt
* 1 tsp. garlic powder
* ½ tsp.f pepper (optional)
* 150 g cheese
* 240 ml milk
* Hot water and cornflour as needed

DIRECTIONS:

1. Stir together all the ingredients except the cheese and milk in your Instant Pot.
2. Lock the lid. Press the Manual button and cook for 3 minutes at High Pressure.
3. Once cooking is complete, use a quick pressure release. Carefully remove the lid.
4. Add the cheese and half and half and stir until the cheese has melted. Let stand for about 5 minutes until thickened.
5. Combine some hot water and some cornflour in a medium bowl and add to the pot to thicken quicker.
6. Serve.

. . . .

FETA AND ROCKET PASTA SALAD

Prep time: 10 minutes | Cook time: 8 minutes | Serves 4 to 6

INGREDIENTS:

* 455 g dry rotini pasta
* Water as needed, to cover the pasta
* 60 g rocket or spinach, chopped
* 245 g feta cheese, diced
* 2 Roma or plum tomatoes, diced
* 2 garlic cloves, minced
* 1 red pepper, diced
* 2 tbsps. white wine vinegar
* 80 ml extra-virgin olive oil
* Salt and ground black pepper, to taste

DIRECTIONS:

1. Place the pasta and water in your Instant Pot.
2. Secure the lid. Press the Manual button on your Instant Pot and set the cooking time for 8 minutes on High Pressure.
3. Once the timer goes off, do a quick pressure release. Carefully open the lid.
4. Drain the pasta and set aside.
5. Mix together the rocket, feta, tomatoes, garlic, pepper, vinegar, and olive oil in a large bowl.
6. Fold in the pasta. Sprinkle with salt and pepper. Stir well.
7. Serve immediately.

CHAPTER 5 VEGETABLES

GRAPE LEAVES AND NUT RICE BOWL

Prep time: 15 minutes | Cook time: 4 minutes | Serves 4

INGREDIENTS:

* 160 g chopped onion
* 140 g chopped tomato
* 200 g basmati rice, rinsed and drained
* 135 g pine nuts
* 230 g brined grape leaves, drained and chopped
* 2 tbsps. olive oil
* 3 cloves garlic, minced
* 1 tbsp. dried parsley
* 1½ tsps. ground allspice
* 1 tsp. salt
* 1 tsp. black pepper
* 240 ml water
* 80 ml fresh lemon juice
* 5 g chopped fresh mint

DIRECTIONS:

1. In the Instant Pot, combine the onion, tomato, rice, pine nuts, grape leaves, olive oil, garlic, parsley, allspice, salt, pepper, and water. Stir to combine.
2. Lock the lid. Select Manual mode and set the timer for 4 minutes on High Pressure.
3. When timer beeps, perform a natural pressure release for 10 minutes, then release any remaining pressure. Open the lid.
4. Stir in the lemon juice and mint and serve.

....

GREEN BEANS WITH COCONUT

Prep time: 10 minutes | Cook time: 3 minutes | Serves 4

INGREDIENTS:

* 2 tbsps. vegetable oil
* 1 tsp. mustard seeds
* 1 tsp. cumin seeds
* 160 g diced onion
* 1 tsp. ground turmeric
* 1 tsp. salt
* ½ tsp. cayenne pepper
* 1 (340-g) package frozen green beans
* 25 g unsweetened shredded coconut
* 120 ml water
* 5 g chopped fresh coriander

DIRECTIONS:

1. Select Sauté mode on the Instant Pot. When the pot is hot, add the oil. Once the oil is hot, add the mustard seeds and cumin seeds, and allow to sizzle for 15 to 20 seconds.
2. Stir in the onion. Add the turmeric, salt, and cayenne and stir to coat. Add the green beans, coconut, and water; stir to combine.
3. Lock the lid. Select Manual mode and set the timer for 2 minutes at High Pressure.
4. When timer beeps, use a quick pressure release. Open the lid.
5. Transfer to a serving dish and garnish with the coriander. Serve warm.

....

GARLICKY BABY BOK CHOY

Prep time: 9 minutes | Cook time: 4 minutes | Serves 6

INGREDIENTS:

* 1 tsp. peanut oil
* 455 g baby Bok choy, trimmed and washed
* Salt and pepper, to taste
* 4 garlic cloves, minced
* 1 tsp. red pepper flakes
* 240 ml water

DIRECTIONS:

1. Press the Sauté button on the Instant Pot.
2. Heat the oil and sauté the garlic for 1 minute until fragrant.
3. Add the Bok choy and sprinkle salt and pepper for seasoning.
4. Pour in the water.
5. Lock the lid. Set the Instant Pot to Manual mode, then set the timer for 4 minutes at High Pressure.
6. Once cooking is complete, do a quick pressure release. Carefully open the lid.
7. Sprinkle with red pepper flakes, then serve.

VEGGIE STEW

Prep time: 6 minutes | Cook time: 10 minutes | Serves 5

INGREDIENTS:

* 70 g chopped tomatoes
* 1 stalk celery, minced
* 2 courgettes, chopped

* 455 g mushrooms, sliced
* 1 onion, chopped
* Salt and pepper, to taste

DIRECTIONS:

1. Place all the ingredients in the Instant Pot.
2. Pour in enough water until half of the vegetables are submerged.
3. Lock the lid. Set the Instant Pot to Manual mode, then set the timer for 10 minutes at High Pressure.
4. Once cooking is complete, do a quick pressure release. Carefully open the lid.
5. Serve warm.

. . . .

COURGETTE STICKS

Prep time: 5 minutes | Cook time: 8 minutes | Serves 2

INGREDIENTS:

* 2 courgettes, trimmed and cut into sticks
* 2 tsps. olive oil
* ½ tsp. white peppe

* ½ tsp. salt
* 240 ml water

DIRECTIONS:

1. Place the courgette sticks in the Instant Pot pan and sprinkle with the olive oil, white pepper and salt.
2. Pour the water and put the trivet in the pot. Place the pan on the trivet.
3. Lock the lid. Select the Manual setting and set the cooking time for 8 minutes at High Pressure. Once the timer goes off, use a quick pressure release. Carefully open the lid.
4. Remove the courgettes from the pot and serve.

. . . .

MUSHROOMS WITH GARLIC

Prep time: 12 minutes | Cook time: 10 minutes | Serves 1

INGREDIENTS:

* 120 ml water
* 100 g mushrooms, sliced
* 2 garlic cloves, minced
* 1 tbsp. olive oil
* Salt and pepper, to taste

DIRECTIONS:

1. Pour water along with mushrooms in an Instant Pot.
2. Lock the lid. Set the Instant Pot to Manual mode, then set the timer for 5 minutes at High Pressure.
3. Once cooking is complete, do a quick pressure release. Carefully open the lid.
4. Drain the mushroom and then return back to the Instant Pot.
5. Now add olive oil to the pot and mix.
6. Press the Sauté function of the pot and let it cook for 3 minutes.
7. Sauté every 30 seconds.
8. Add the garlic and sauté for 2 minutes or until fragrant. Sprinkle with salt and pepper, then serve the dish.

STEAMED ASPARAGUS

Prep time: 5minutes | Cook time: 5 minutes | Serves 1

INGREDIENTS:

* 7 asparagus spears, washed and trimmed
* ¼ tsp. pepper
* 1 tbsp. extra virgin olive oil
* Juice from freshly squeezed ¼ lemon
* ¼ tsp. salt
* 240 ml water

DIRECTIONS:

1. Place a trivet or the steamer rack in the Instant Pot and pour in the water.
2. In a mixing bowl, combine the asparagus spears, salt, pepper, and lemon juice.
3. Place on top of the trivet.
4. Lock the lid. Set the Instant Pot to Steam mode, then set the timer for 5 minutes at High Pressure.
5. Once cooking is complete, do a quick pressure release. Carefully open the lid.
6. Drizzle the asparagus with olive oil.

RATATOUILLE

Prep time: 20 minutes | Cook time: 10 minutes | Serves 4

INGREDIENTS:

* 480 ml water
* 2 medium courgette, sliced
* 3 tomatoes, sliced
* 2 aubergines, sliced
* 1 tbsp. olive oil
* Salt and pepper, to taste

DIRECTIONS:

1. Pour the water into the Instant Pot.
2. In a baking dish, arrange a layer of the courgette.
3. Top with a layer of the tomatoes.
4. Place a layer of aubergine slices on top.
5. Continue layering until you use all the ingredients.
6. Drizzle with olive oil.
7. Place the baking dish on the trivet and lower it.
8. Lock the lid. Set the Instant Pot to Manual mode, then set the timer for 10 minutes at High Pressure.
9. Once cooking is complete, do a quick pressure release. Carefully open the lid.
10. Sprinkle with salt and pepper and serve warm!

BROCCOLI WITH ROASTED ALMONDS

Prep time: 10 minutes | Cook time: 4 minutes | Serves 4 to 6

INGREDIENTS:

* 530 g broccoli florets
* 240 ml water
* 1½ tbsps. olive oil
* 8 garlic cloves, thinly sliced
* 2 shallots, thinly sliced
* ½ tsp. crushed red pepper flakes
* Grated zest and juice of 1 medium lemon
* ½ tsp. salt
* Freshly ground black pepper, to taste
* 25 g chopped roasted almonds
* 10 g finely slivered fresh basil

DIRECTIONS:

1. Pour the water into the Instant Pot. Place the broccoli florets in a steamer basket and lower into the pot.
2. Close and secure the lid. Select the Steam setting and set the cooking time for 2 minutes at Low Pressure. Once the timer goes off, use a quick pressure release. Carefully open the lid.
3. Transfer the broccoli to a large bowl filled with cold water and ice. Once cooled, drain the broccoli and pat dry.
4. Select the Sauté mode on the Instant Pot and heat the olive oil. Add the garlic to the pot and sauté for 30 seconds, tossing constantly. Add the shallots and pepper flakes to the pot and sauté for 1 minute.
5. Stir in the cooked broccoli, lemon juice, salt and black pepper. Toss the ingredients together and cook for 1 minute.
6. Transfer the broccoli to a serving platter and sprinkle with the chopped almonds, lemon zest and basil. Serve immediately.

ARTICHOKES WITH ONION

Prep time: 6 minutes | Cook time: 30 minutes | Serves 8

INGREDIENTS:

* 120 ml organic chicken stock
* Salt and pepper, to taste
* 4 large artichokes, trimmed and cleaned
* 1 onion, chopped
* 1 garlic clove, crushed

DIRECTIONS:

1. Place all ingredients in the Instant Pot.
2. Lock the lid. Set the Instant Pot to Manual mode, then set the timer for 30 minutes at High Pressure.
3. Once cooking is complete, do a quick pressure release. Carefully open the lid.
4. Serve the artichokes with lemon juice.

. . . .

ITALIAN CARROT AND POTATO MEDLEY

Prep time: 15 minutes | Cook time: 11 minutes | Serves 4

INGREDIENTS:

* 2 tbsps. olive oil
* 150 g potatoes, peeled and chopped
* 3 carrots, peeled and chopped
* 3 garlic cloves, minced
* 240 ml vegetable stock
* 1 tsp. Italian seasoning
* Salt and black pepper, to taste
* 1 tbsp. chopped parsley
* 1 tbsp. chopped oregano

DIRECTIONS:

1. Set the Instant Pot to the Sauté mode. Heat the olive oil until shimmering.
2. Add and sauté the potatoes and carrots for 5 minutes or until tender.
3. Add the garlic and cook for a minute or until fragrant. Pour in the vegetable stock, season with Italian seasoning, salt, and black pepper.
4. Seal the lid. Select the Manual mode and set the time for 5 minutes at High Pressure.
5. Once cooking is complete, do a quick pressure release, then unlock the lid.
6. Spoon the potatoes and carrots into a serving bowl and mix in the parsley and oregano. Serve warm.

. . . .

GARLICKY BABY POTATOES

Prep time: 30 minutes | Cook time: 11 minutes | Serves 4

INGREDIENTS:

* 1 tbsp. olive oil
* 3 garlic cloves
* 900 g baby potatoes
* 1 sprig rosemary
* 240 ml vegetable stock
* Salt and pepper, to taste

DIRECTIONS:

1. Hit the Sauté button in the Instant Pot.
2. Add the olive oil.
3. Add the garlic, baby potatoes and rosemary.
4. Brown the outside of the potatoes.
5. Pierce each potato with a fork.
6. Add the vegetable stock.
7. Lock the lid. Set the Instant Pot to Manual mode, then set the timer for 11 minutes at High Pressure.
8. Once cooking is complete, do a quick pressure release. Carefully open the lid.
9. Season with salt and pepper and serve.

CAULIFLOWER TOTS

Prep time: 30 minutes | Cook time: 10 minutes | Serves 4

INGREDIENTS:

* 240 ml water
* 1 large cauliflower
* 1 egg, beaten
* 100 g almond meal
* 100 g grated Parmesan cheese
* 100 g grated Gruyere cheese
* 2 garlic cloves, minced
* Salt, to taste
* 3 tbsps. olive oil

DIRECTIONS:

1. Pour the water in the Instant Pot, then fit in a trivet and place the cauliflower on top.
2. Seal the lid. Select the Manual mode and set the time for 3 minutes at High Pressure.
3. Once cooking is complete, do a quick pressure release. Carefully open the lid.
4. Transfer the cauliflower to a food processor and pulse to rice the cauliflower.
5. Pour the cauliflower rice into a bowl. Mix in the egg, almond meal, cheeses, garlic, and salt.
6. Make the tots: Form the mixture into 5 cm oblong balls. Place on a baking sheet and chill in the refrigerator for 20 minutes.
7. Set the Instant Pot on Sauté mode. Heat the olive oil until shimmering.
8. Remove tots from refrigerator and fry in the oil for 6 minutes on all sides until golden brown. Flip the tots in the oil during the frying. Work in batches to avoid overcrowding.
9. Place the tots on a paper towel-lined plate to pat dry and serve.

GOBI MASALA

Prep time: 5 minutes | Cook time: 4 to 5 minutes | Serves 4 to 6

INGREDIENTS:

* 1 tbsp. olive oil
* 1 tsp. cumin seeds
* 1 white onion, diced
* 1 garlic clove, minced
* 1 head cauliflower, chopped
* 1 tbsp. ground coriander
* 1 tsp. ground cumin
* ½ tsp. garam masala
* ½ tsp. salt
* 240 ml water

DIRECTIONS:

1. Set the Instant Pot to the Sauté mode and heat the olive oil. Add the cumin seeds to the pot and sauté for 30 seconds, stirring constantly. Add the onion and sauté for 2 to 3 minutes, stirring constantly. Add the garlic and sauté for 30 seconds, stirring frequently.
2. Stir in the remaining ingredients.
3. Lock the lid. Select the Manual mode and set the cooking time for 1 minute on High Pressure. When the timer goes off, perform a quick pressure release. Carefully open the lid.
4. Serve immediately.

VEGETABLE BURGERS

Prep time: 20 minutes | Cook time: 55 minutes | Serves 2

INGREDIENTS:

* 2 tbsps. olive oil, divided
* ½ medium red pepper, deseeded and chopped
* ½ medium yellow onion, chopped
* ½ medium courgette, chopped
* 55 g chopped yellow squash
* 4 cloves garlic, minced
* 195 g dried black beans
* 1.9 L water
* 1 tsp. salt
* 55 g panko bread crumbs
* ½ jalapeño, deseeded and minced
* Pinch freshly ground black pepper
* 2 burger buns

DIRECTIONS:

1. Press the Sauté button on the Instant Pot and heat 1 tbsp. of olive oil until shimmering.
2. Add the pepper and onion and sauté for 3 minutes or until the onion is translucent.
3. Add the courgette, squash, and garlic and sauté for 3 minutes. Transfer the vegetables in the pot to a small bowl and set aside.
4. Add the beans, water, and salt to the pot. Lock the lid. Press the Bean button and set the cooking time for 30 minutes at High Pressure.
5. When the timer beeps, let pressure release naturally for 10 minutes. Release any remaining pressure, then unlock lid.
6. Press the Sauté button on the pot and simmer bean mixture for 10 minutes to thicken.
7. Transfer the mixture to a large bowl and mash with forks. When cool enough to handle, quickly mix in the vegetable mixture, panko, jalapeño, and pepper and blend thoroughly.
8. Form the mixture into 2 patties. Cook in a frying pan over remaining 1 tbsp. of olive oil for 2 to 3 minutes on each side until browned.
9. Remove from heat and assemble each patty with a bun. Serve warm.

CHAPTER 6 POULTRY

BRUSCHETTA CHICKEN

Prep time: 5 minutes | Cook time: 20 minutes | Serves 2

INGREDIENTS:

* 120 ml filtered water
* 2 boneless, skinless chicken breasts
* 1 (400-g) can sugar-free or low-sugar crushed tomatoes
* ¼ tsp. dried basil
* 50 g shredded full-fat Cheddar cheese
* 60 g heavy whipping cream

DIRECTIONS:

1. Add the filtered water, chicken breasts, tomatoes, and basil to your Instant Pot.
2. Lock the lid. Press the Manual button and set the cooking time for 20 minutes on High Pressure.
3. Once cooking is complete, use a quick pressure release. Carefully open the lid.
4. Fold in the cheese and cream and stir until the cheese is melted.
5. Serve immediately.

INDIAN BUTTER CHICKEN

Prep time: 10 minutes | Cook time: 15 minutes | Serves 4

INGREDIENTS:

* 3 tbsps. butter or ghee, at room temperature, divided
* 1 medium yellow onion, halved and sliced through the root end
* 1 (285 g) can tomatoes with green chilies, with juice
* 2 tbsps. mild Indian curry paste
* 680 g boneless, skinless chicken thighs, fat trimmed, cut into 5 cm pieces
* 2 tbsps. plain flour
* Salt and freshly ground black pepper, to taste

DIRECTIONS:

1. Add 1 tbsp. of the butter in the Instant Pot and select the Sauté mode. Add the onion and sauté for 6 minutes until browned.
2. Stir in the tomatoes and scrape any browned bits from the pot. Add the curry paste and stir well. Fold in the chicken and stir to coat.
3. Secure the lid. Press the Manual button on the Instant Pot and cook for 8 minutes on High Pressure.
4. Once cooking is complete, use a quick pressure release.
5. Combine the remaining 2 tbsps. of butter and the flour in a small bowl and stir until smooth.
6. Select the Sauté mode. Add the flour mixture to the chicken in two additions, stirring between additions. Sauté for 1 minute, or until the sauce is thickened.
7. Sprinkle with the salt and pepper and serve.

LEMON GARLIC CHICKEN

Prep time: 1 hour 20 minutes | Cook time: 12 minutes | Serves 6

INGREDIENTS:

* 3 tbsps. olive oil, divided
* 2 tsps. dried parsley
* 6 chicken breasts
* 3 minced garlic cloves
* 1 tbsp. lemon juice
* Salt and pepper, to taste

DIRECTIONS:

1. Mix together 2 tbsps. olive oil, chicken breasts, parsley, garlic cloves, and lemon juice in a large bowl. Place in the refrigerator to marinate for 1 hour.
2. Press the Sauté button on the Instant Pot and heat the remaining olive oil.
3. Cook the chicken breasts for 5 to 6 minutes per side until cooked through.
4. Allow to cool for 5 minutes before serving.

MONGOLIAN CHICKEN

Prep time: 5 minutes | Cook time: 20 minutes | Serves 6

INGREDIENTS:

* 2 tbsps. olive oil
* 10 cloves garlic, minced
* 1 onion, minced
* 4 large boneless, skinless chicken breasts, cut into cubes
* 240 ml water
* 240 ml soy sauce

* 210 g brown sugar
* 100 g chopped carrots
* 1 tbsp. garlic powder
* 1 tbsp. grated ginger
* 1 tsp. red pepper flakes
* 1 tbsp. cornflour, mixed with 2 tbsps. water

DIRECTIONS:

1. Set your Instant Pot to Sauté and heat the olive oil.
2. Add the garlic and onion and sauté for about 3 minutes until fragrant.
3. Add the chicken cubes and brown each side for 3 minutes. Add the remaining ingredients except the cornflour mixture to the Instant Pot and stir well.
4. Secure the lid. Select the Poultry mode and set the cooking time for 15 minutes at High Pressure.
5. Once cooking is complete, do a natural pressure release for 10 minutes, then release any remaining pressure. Carefully open the lid.
6. Set your Instant Pot to Sauté again and whisk in the cornflour mixture until the sauce thickens.
7. Serve warm.

. . . .

ORANGE CHICKEN BREASTS

Prep time: 5 minutes | Cook time: 18 minutes | Serves 4

INGREDIENTS:

* 4 chicken breasts
* 205 g orange marmalade
* 180 g barbecue sauce
* 60 ml water

* 2 tbsps. soy sauce
* 1 tbsp. cornflour, mixed with 2 tbsps. water
* 2 tbsps. green onions, chopped

DIRECTIONS:

1. Combine all the ingredients except the cornflour mixture and green onions in the Instant Pot.
2. Secure the lid. Select the Poultry mode and set the cooking time for 15 minutes at High Pressure.
3. Once cooking is complete, do a quick pressure release. Carefully open the lid.
4. Set your Instant Pot to Sauté and stir in the cornflour mixture. Simmer for a few minutes until the sauce is thickened.
5. Add the green onions and stir well. Serve immediately.

. . . .

JAMAICAN CURRY CHICKEN DRUMSTICKS

Prep time: 5 minutes | Cook time: 20 minutes | Serves 4

INGREDIENTS:

* 680 g chicken drumsticks
* 1 tbsp. Jamaican curry powder
* 1 tsp. salt
* 240 ml chicken stock
* ½ medium onion, diced
* ½ tsp. dried thyme

DIRECTIONS:

1. Sprinkle the salt and curry powder over the chicken drumsticks.
2. Place the chicken drumsticks into the Instant Pot, along with the remaining ingredients.
3. Secure the lid. Select the Manual mode and set the cooking time for 20 minutes at High Pressure.
4. Once cooking is complete, do a quick pressure release. Carefully open the lid. Serve warm.

INSTANT POT RANCH CHICKEN

Prep time: 5 minutes | Cook time: 20 minutes | Serves 6

INGREDIENTS:

* 1 tsp. salt
* ½ tsp. garlic powder
* ¼ tsp. pepper
* ¼ tsp. dried oregano
* 3 (170-g) skinless chicken breasts
* 115 g butter
* 230 g cream cheese
* 1 dry ranch packet
* 240 ml chicken stock

DIRECTIONS:

1. In a small bowl, combine the salt, garlic powder, pepper, and oregano. Rub this mixture over both sides of chicken breasts.
2. Place the chicken breasts into the Instant Pot, along with the butter, cream cheese, ranch seasoning, and chicken stock.
3. Secure the lid. Select the Manual mode and set the cooking time for 20 minutes at High Pressure.
4. Once cooking is complete, do a natural pressure release for 10 minutes, then release any remaining pressure. Carefully open the lid.
5. Remove the chicken and shred with two forks, then return to the Instant Pot. Use a rubber spatula to stir and serve on a plate.

CHICKEN ENCHILADA BOWL

Prep time: 10 minutes | Cook time: 35 minutes | Serves 4

INGREDIENTS:

* 2 (170-g) boneless, skinless chicken breasts
* 2 tsps. chili powder
* ½ tsp. garlic powder
* ½ tsp. salt
* ¼ tsp. pepper
* 2 tbsps. coconut oil
* 180 g red enchilada sauce
* 60 ml chicken stock
* 1 (115 g) can green chilies
* 40 g diced onion
* 215 g cooked cauliflower rice
* 1 avocado, diced
* 120 g sour cream
* 100 g shredded Cheddar cheese

DIRECTIONS:

1. Sprinkle the chili powder, garlic powder, salt, and pepper on chicken breasts.
2. Set your Instant Pot to Sauté and melt the coconut oil. Add the chicken breasts and sear each side for about 5 minutes until golden brown.
3. Pour the enchilada sauce and stock over the chicken. Using a wooden spoon or rubber spatula, scrape the bottom of pot to make sure nothing is sticking. Stir in the chilies and onion.
4. Secure the lid. Select the Manual mode and set the cooking time for 25 minutes at High Pressure.
5. Once cooking is complete, do a quick pressure release. Carefully open the lid.
6. Remove the chicken and shred with two forks. Serve the chicken over the cauliflower rice and place the avocado, sour cream, and Cheddar cheese on top.

PAPRIKA CHICKEN WITH TOMATOES

Prep time: 10 minutes | Cook time: 20 minutes | Serves 4

INGREDIENTS:

* 1 tbsp. avocado oil
* 675 g chicken breast, skinless, boneless, and cubed
* 150 g tomatoes, cubed
* 240 ml chicken stock
* 1 tbsp. smoked paprika
* 1 tsp. cayenne pepper
* A pinch of salt and black pepper

DIRECTIONS:

1. Set your Instant Pot to Sauté and heat the oil. Cook the cubed chicken in the hot oil for 2 to 3 minutes until lightly browned.
2. Add the remaining ingredients to the pot and stir well.
3. Lock the lid. Select the Poultry mode and set the cooking time for 18 minutes at High Pressure.
4. Once cooking is complete, do a natural pressure release for 10 minutes, then release any remaining pressure. Carefully open the lid.
5. Serve the chicken and tomatoes in bowls while warm.

HONEY-GLAZED CHICKEN WITH SESAME

Prep time: 5 minutes | Cook time: 25 minutes | Serves 6

INGREDIENTS:

* 1 tbsp. olive oil
* 2 cloves garlic, minced
* 80 g diced onions
* 4 large boneless, skinless chicken breasts
* Salt and pepper, to taste
* 120 ml soy sauce

* 170 g honey
* 60 g ketchup
* 2 tsps. sesame oil
* ¼ tsp. red pepper flakes
* 2 green onions, chopped
* 1 tbsp. sesame seeds, toasted

DIRECTIONS:

1. Press the Sauté button on the Instant Pot and heat the olive oil.
2. Add the garlic and onions and sauté for about 3 minutes until fragrant.
3. Add the chicken breasts and sprinkle with the salt and pepper. Brown each side for 3 minutes.
4. Stir in the soy sauce, honey, ketchup, sesame oil, and red pepper flakes.
5. Secure the lid. Select the Poultry mode and set the cooking time for 20 minutes at High Pressure.
6. Once cooking is complete, do a natural pressure release for 10 minutes, then release any remaining pressure. Carefully open the lid.
7. Sprinkle the onions and sesame seeds on top for garnish before serving.

- -

HULI HULI CHICKEN

Prep time: 5 minutes | Cook time: 10 minutes | Serves 8

INGREDIENTS:

* 175 g crushed pineapple, drained
* 60 ml reduced-sodium soy sauce
* 180 g ketchup
* 3 tbsps. lime juice

* 3 tbsps. packed brown sugar
* 1 garlic clove, minced
* 8 boneless, skinless chicken thighs, about 910 g
* Hot cooked rice, for serving

DIRECTIONS:

1. Mix together the pineapple, soy sauce, ketchup, lime juice, sugar, and clove in a mixing bowl.
2. Add the chicken to your Instant Pot and place the mixture on top.
3. Secure the lid. Press the Manual button on the Instant Pot and set the cooking time for 10 minutes at High Pressure.
4. Once cooking is complete, use a natural pressure release for 5 minutes and then release any remaining pressure. Carefully open the lid.
5. Serve with the cooked rice.

- -

LEMONY CHICKEN WITH POTATOES

Prep time: 5 minutes | Cook time: 21 minutes | Serves 4

INGREDIENTS:

* 910 g chicken thighs
* 1 tsp. fine sea salt
* ½ tsp. ground black pepper
* 2 tbsps. olive oil

* 60 ml freshly squeezed lemon juice
* 180 ml low-sodium chicken stock
* 2 tbsps. Italian seasoning
* 2 to 3 tbsps. Dijon mustard
* 910 g to 1.3 kg red potatoes, quartered

DIRECTIONS:

1. Sprinkle the chicken with the salt and pepper.
2. Add the oil to your Instant Pot. Select the Sauté mode. Add the chicken and sauté for 3 minutes until browned on both sides.
3. Meanwhile, make the sauce by stirring together the lemon juice, chicken stock, Italian seasoning, and mustard in a medium mixing bowl.
4. Drizzle the sauce over the chicken. Fold in the potatoes.
5. Secure the lid. Press the Manual button on the Instant Pot and cook for 15 minutes on High Pressure.
6. Once cooking is complete, do a quick pressure release. Carefully remove the lid.
7. Transfer the chicken to a serving dish and serve immediately.

MEXICAN SHREDDED CHICKEN

Prep time: 12 minutes | Cook time: 18 minutes | Serves 4

INGREDIENTS:

* ½ tsp. paprika
* 1.3 kg chicken breasts
* ½ tsp. dried oregano
* 1 tbsp. chili powder
* ¼ tsp. cumin powder
* Salt and pepper, to taste
* 480 ml water

DIRECTIONS:

1. Place all ingredients in the Instant Pot and whisk well.
2. Lock the lid. Select the Poultry mode and set the cooking time for 18 minutes at High Pressure.
3. Once cooking is complete, do a natural pressure release for 12 minutes, then release any remaining pressure. Carefully open the lid.
4. Remove the chicken breasts from the pot and shred them. Serve immediately.

· ·

LEMONY FENNEL CHICKEN

Prep time: 12 minutes | Cook time: 12 minutes | Serves 8

INGREDIENTS:

* 3 tbsps. freshly squeezed lemon juice
* 1 tsp. cinnamon
* 20 g fennel bulb
* 4 garlic cloves, minced
* 900 g boneless and skinless chicken thighs
* Salt and pepper, to taste
* 120 ml water

DIRECTIONS:

1. Place lemon juice, cinnamon, fennel bulb, garlic, and chicken thighs in the Instant Pot. Sprinkle pepper and salt for seasoning. Add 120 ml of water for moisture.
2. Lock the lid. Select the Manual mode and cook for 12 minutes at High Pressure.
3. Once cooking is complete, do a natural pressure release for 8 minutes, then release any remaining pressure. Carefully open the lid.
4. Remove the chicken from the pot and shred it, then serve.

· ·

KALE CHICKEN SOUP

Prep time: 3 minutes | Cook time: 18 minutes | Serves 8

INGREDIENTS:

* 680 g chicken breasts
* 1.2 L water
* 150 g chopped tomatoes
* 2 cloves garlic, minced
* 1 onion, chopped
* 1 thumb-size ginger
* Salt and pepper, to taste
* 60 g kale leaves

DIRECTIONS:

1. Combine all the ingredients except the kale leaves in the Instant Pot.
2. Secure the lid. Select the Poultry mode and set the cooking time for 15 minutes at High Pressure.
3. Once cooking is complete, do a natural pressure release for 10 minutes, then release any remaining pressure. Carefully open the lid.
4. Set your Instant Pot to Sauté and stir in the kale leaves. Allow to simmer for 3 minutes until softened.
5. Divide into bowls and serve warm.

CHAPTER 7 PORK, BEEF AND LAMB

PORK WITH PEPPERS

Prep time: 10 minutes | Cook time: 35 minutes | Serves 4

INGREDIENTS:

* 2 tbsps. olive oil
* 4 pork chops
* 1 red onion, chopped
* 3 garlic cloves, minced
* 1 red pepper, roughly chopped
* 1 green pepper, roughly chopped
* 480 ml beef stock
* A pinch of salt and black pepper
* 1 tbsp. parsley, chopped

DIRECTIONS:

1. Press the Sauté on your Instant Pot. Add and heat the oil. Brown the pork chops for 2 minutes.
2. Fold in the onion and garlic and brown for an additional 3 minutes.
3. Stir in the peppers, stock, salt, and pepper.
4. Lock the lid. Select the Manual mode and cook for 30 minutes on High Pressure.
5. Once cooking is complete, use a natural pressure release for 10 minutes and then release any remaining pressure. Carefully open the lid.
6. Divide the mix among the plates and serve topped with the parsley.

. . . .

PORK WITH BRUSSELS SPROUTS

Prep time: 10 minutes | Cook time: 30 minutes | Serves 4

INGREDIENTS:

* 680 g pork chops
* 455 g Brussels sprouts, trimmed and halved
* 2 tbsps. Cajun seasoning
* 240 ml beef stock
* A pinch of salt and black peppe
* 1 tbsp. parsley, chopped

DIRECTIONS:

1. Stir together all the ingredients in your Instant Pot.
2. Secure the lid. Press the Manual button on the Instant Pot and set the cooking time for 30 minutes on High Pressure.
3. Once cooking is complete, perform a natural pressure release for 10 minutes and then release any remaining pressure. Carefully open the lid.
4. Divide the mix among the plates and serve immediately.

. . . .

PORK WITH MUSHROOM SAUCE

Prep time: 10 minutes | Cook time: 15 minutes | Serves 2

INGREDIENTS:

* 1 tbsp. oil
* 2 bone-in, medium-cut pork chops
* Salt and freshly ground black pepper, to taste
* 115 g cremini mushrooms, sliced
* 2 garlic cloves, minced
* ½ small onion, sliced
* Splash of dry white wine
* 240 ml chicken stock
* 1 tbsp. cornflour
* 1 tbsp. butter
* 180 g sour cream

DIRECTIONS:

1. Set your Instant Pot to Sauté. Add and heat the oil.
2. Sprinkle the pork chops generously with the salt and pepper. Sear the pork chops on both sides and transfer to a plate.
3. Add the mushrooms, garlic, and onion and sauté for 3 minutes until soft. Add the white wine and deglaze the pot by scraping up any browned bits on the bottom with a wooden spoon.
4. Stir in the stock. Add the seared pork chops to the pot.
5. Lock the lid. Select the Manual mode and cook for 8 minutes on High Pressure.
6. Once cooking is complete, do a natural pressure release for about 10 minutes. Carefully open the lid.
7. Select the Sauté mode.
8. Transfer the pork chops to a plate. Remove 1 tbsp. of the cooking liquid from the pot and pour in a small bowl with the cornflour. Stir well and transfer the mixture back to the pot.
9. Mix in the butter and sour cream and stir until mixed. Let simmer for 4 to 5 minutes until thickened. Sprinkle with the salt and pepper if necessary.
10. Transfer to a serving plate and serve.

PORK CHOPS WITH ONIONS

Prep time: 10 minutes | Cook time: 35 minutes | Serves 4

INGREDIENTS:

* 3 tbsps. butter
* 4 boneless pork chops
* 3 onions, chopped
* 120 ml beef stock
* Salt and pepper, to taste
* 60 g heavy cream

DIRECTIONS:

1. Press the Sauté button on the Instant Pot.
2. Heat the butter until melted and add the pork chops and onion.
3. Sauté for 3 minutes or until the pork is seared.
4. Stir in the stock and sprinkle salt and pepper for seasoning.
5. Lock the lid. Press the Meat/Stew button and set the cooking time to 20 minutes at High Pressure.
6. Once cooking is complete, perform a natural pressure release for 10 minutes, and then release any remaining pressure. Carefully open the lid.
7. Add the heavy cream. Press the Sauté button and allow to simmer for 5 minutes.
8. Allow to cool for a few minutes. Remove the pork from the pot and serve warm.

PORK CHOPS WITH SAUERKRAUT

Prep time: 15 minutes | Cook time: 30 minutes | Serves 4

INGREDIENTS:

* 2 tbsps. olive oil
* 4 (2.5 cm thick) bone-in pork loin chops
* 1 tsp. sea salt
* ½ tsp. ground black pepper
* 4 slices bacon, diced
* 3 large carrots, peeled and sliced
* 1 large onion, peeled and diced
* 1 stalk celery, finely chopped
* 1 clove garlic, peeled and minced
* 1 (340-g) bottle lager
* 2 medium red apples, peeled, cored, and quartered
* 4 medium red potatoes, peeled and quartered
* 1 (455-g) bag high-quality sauerkraut, rinsed and drained
* 1 tbsp. caraway seeds

DIRECTIONS:

1. Set your Instant Pot to Sauté. Add and heat the olive oil.
2. Sprinkle the pork chops with the salt and pepper. Working in batches, sear the pork chops for 1 to 2 minutes on each side. Set aside.
3. Add the bacon, carrots, onion, and celery to the Instant Pot. Sauté for 3 to 5 minutes, or until the onions are translucent.
4. Fold in the garlic and cook for an additional 1 minute. Pour in the beer and deglaze the bottom of the pot by scraping out any browned bits from the pot. Let simmer uncovered for 5 minutes.
5. Mix in the apples, potatoes, and sauerkraut. Sprinkle the caraway seeds on top. Slightly prop pork chops up against the sides of the pot to avoid crowding the pork.
6. Secure the lid. Select the Manual function and cook for 15 minutes on High Pressure.
7. Once the timer goes off, do a natural pressure release for 5 minutes and release any remaining pressure. Carefully remove the lid.
8. Transfer to a serving plate and serve immediately.

LEMON BEEF MEAL

Prep time: 12 minutes | Cook time: 10 minutes | Serves 2

INGREDIENTS:

* 1 tbsp. olive oil
* 2 beef steaks
* ½ tsp. garlic salt
* 1 garlic clove, crushed
* 2 tbsps. lemon juice

DIRECTIONS:

1. Press Sauté on the Instant Pot. Heat the olive oil in the pot until shimmering.
2. Add the beef and garlic salt and sauté for 4 to 5 minutes to evenly brown.
3. Add the garlic and sauté for 1 minute until fragrant.
4. Serve with lemon juice on top.

MONGOLIAN GLAZED BEEF

Prep time: 15 minutes | Cook time: 20 minutes | Serves 4

INGREDIENTS:

* 1 tbsp. sesame oil
* 1 (910 g) skirt steak, sliced into thin strips
* 160 g pure maple syrup
* 60 ml soy sauce
* 4 cloves garlic, minced
* 2.5 cm knob fresh ginger root, peeled and grated
* 120 ml plus 2 tbsps. water, divided
* 2 tbsps. cornflour

DIRECTIONS:

1. Press the Sauté button on the Instant Pot. Heat the sesame oil.
2. Add and sear the steak strips for 3 minutes on all sides.
3. In a medium bowl, whisk together maple syrup, soy sauce, garlic, ginger, and 120 ml water. Pour the mixture over beef. Lock the lid.
4. Press the Manual button and set the cooking time for 10 minutes at High Pressure.
5. When timer beeps, quick release the pressure, then unlock the lid.
6. Meanwhile, in a small dish, whisk together the arrowroot and 2 tbsps. water until smooth and chunky.
7. Stir the cornflour into the beef mixture. Press the Sauté button and simmer for 5 minutes or until the sauce thickens.
8. Ladle the beef and sauce on plates and serve.

KOREAN BEEF RIBS

Prep time: 10 minutes | Cook time: 15 minutes | Serves 6

INGREDIENTS:

* 1.4 kg beef short ribs
* 240 ml beef stock
* 2 green onions, sliced
* 1 tbsp. toasted sesame seeds

Sauce:

* ½ tsp. gochujang
* 120 ml rice wine
* 120 ml soy sauce
* ½ tsp. garlic powder
* 160 g pure maple syrup
* 1 tsp. white pepper
* 1 tbsp. sesame oil

DIRECTIONS:

1. In a large bowl, combine the ingredients for the sauce. Dunk the rib in the bowl and press to coat well. Cover the bowl in plastic and refrigerate for at least an hour.
2. Add the beef stock to the Instant Pot. Insert a trivet. Arrange the ribs standing upright over the trivet. Lock the lid.
3. Press the Manual button and set the cooking time for 25 minutes at High Pressure.
4. When timer beeps, let pressure release naturally for 10 minutes, then release any remaining pressure. Unlock the lid.
5. Transfer ribs to a serving platter and garnish with green onions and sesame seeds. Serve immediately.

LEMONGRASS RICE AND BEEF POT

Prep time: 45 minutes | Cook time: 15 minutes | Serves 4

INGREDIENTS:

* 455 g beef stew meat, cut into cubes
* 2 tbsps. olive oil
* 1 green pepper, chopped
* 1 red pepper, chopped
* 1 lemongrass stalk, sliced
* 1 onion, chopped
* 2 garlic cloves, minced
* 200 g jasmine rice
* 480 ml chicken stock
* 2 tbsps. chopped parsley, for garnish

Marinade:

* 1 tbsp. rice wine
* ½ tsp. Five-spice
* ½ tsp. miso paste
* 1 tsp. garlic purée
* 1 tsp. chili powder
* 1 tsp. cumin powder
* 1 tbsp. soy sauce
* 1 tsp. plus ½ tbsp. ginger paste, divided
* ½ tsp. sesame oil
* Salt and black pepper, to taste

DIRECTIONS:

1. In a bowl, add beef and top with the ingredients for the marinade. Mix and wrap the bowl in plastic. Marinate in the refrigerate for 30 minutes.
2. Set the Instant Pot to Sauté mode, then heat the olive oil.
3. Drain beef from marinade and brown in the pot for 5 minutes. Flip frequently.
4. Stir in peppers, lemongrass, onion, and garlic. Sauté for 3 minutes.
5. Stir in rice, cook for 1 minute. Pour in the stock. Seal the lid, select the Manual mode and set the time for 5 minutes on High Pressure.
6. When timer beeps, perform a quick pressure release. Carefully open the lid.
7. Dish out and garnish with parsley. Serve warm.

. . . .

MEXICAN BEEF SHRED

Prep time: 20 minutes | Cook time: 30 minutes | Serves 4

INGREDIENTS:

* 455 g tender chuck roast, cut into half
* 3 tbsps. chipotle sauce
* 1 (230-g) can tomato sauce
* 240 ml beef stock
* 15 g chopped coriander
* 1 lime, zested and juiced
* 2 tsps. cumin powder
* 1 tsp. cayenne pepper
* Salt and ground black pepper, to taste
* ½ tsp. garlic powder
* 1 tbsp. olive oil

DIRECTIONS:

1. In the Instant Pot, add the beef, chipotle sauce, tomato sauce, beef stock, coriander, lime zest, lime juice, cumin powder, cayenne pepper, salt, pepper, and garlic powder.
2. Seal the lid, then select the Manual mode and set the cooking time for 30 minutes at High Pressure.
3. Once cooking is complete, allow a natural pressure release for 10 minutes, then release any remaining pressure.
4. Unlock the lid and using two forks to shred the beef into strands. Stir in the olive oil. Serve warm.

GREEK LAMB LOAF

Prep time: 5 minutes | Cook time: 15 minutes | Serves 2

INGREDIENTS:

* 455 g lamb mincemeat
* 4 garlic cloves
* ½ small onion, chopped
* 1 tsp. ground marjoram
* 1 tsp. rosemary
* ¾ tsp. salt
* ¼ tsp. black pepper
* 180 ml water

DIRECTIONS:

1. In a blender, combine the lamb meat, garlic, onions, marjoram, rosemary, salt and pepper. Pulse until well mixed. Shape the lamb mixture into a compact loaf and cover tightly with aluminum foil. Use a fork to make some holes.
2. Pour the water into the Instant Pot and put a trivet in the pot. Place the lamb loaf on the trivet and lock the lid.
3. Select the Manual mode and set the cooking time for 15 minutes on High Pressure. When the timer goes off, use a quick pressure release.
4. Carefully open the lid. Serve warm.

. . . .

LAMB BURGERS

Prep time: 10 minutes | Cook time: 14 minutes | Serves 2

INGREDIENTS:

* 285 g lamb mince
* ½ tsp. chili powder
* 1 tsp. dried coriander
* 1 tsp. garlic powder
* ½ tsp. salt
* 60 ml water
* 1 tbsp. coconut oil

DIRECTIONS:

1. In a mixing bowl, mix the lamb mince, chili powder, dried coriander, garlic powder, salt, and water.
2. Shape the mixture into 2 burgers.
3. Melt the coconut oil on Sauté mode.
4. Put the burgers in the hot oil and cook for 7 minutes on each side or until well browned.
5. Serve immediately.

. . . .

HARISSA LAMB

Prep time: 30 minutes | Cook time: 40 minutes | Serves 4

INGREDIENTS:

* 1 tbsp. Harissa sauce
* 1 tsp. dried thyme
* ½ tsp. salt
* ½ tsp. salt
* 455 g lamb shoulder
* 2 tbsps. sesame oil
* 480 ml water

DIRECTIONS:

1. In a bowl, mix the Harissa, dried thyme, and salt.
2. Rub the lamb shoulder with the Harissa mixture and brush with sesame oil.
3. Heat the Instant Pot on Sauté mode for 2 minutes and put the lamb shoulder inside.
4. Cook the lamb for 3 minutes on each side, then pour in the water.
5. Close the lid. Select Manual mode and set cooking time for 40 minutes on High Pressure.
6. When timer beeps, use a natural pressure release for 25 minutes, then release any remaining pressure. Open the lid.
7. Serve warm.

GREEK LAMB LEG

Prep time: 10 minutes | Cook time: 50 minutes | Serves 4

INGREDIENTS:

* 455 g lamb leg
* ½ tsp. dried thyme
* 1 tsp. paprika powder
* ¼ tsp. cumin seeds
* 1 tbsp. softened butter
* 2 garlic cloves
* 60 ml water

DIRECTIONS:

1. Rub the lamb leg with dried thyme, paprika powder, and cumin seeds on a clean work surface.
2. Brush the leg with softened butter and transfer to the Instant Pot. Add garlic cloves and water.
3. Close the lid. Select Manual mode and set cooking time for 50 minutes on High Pressure.
4. When timer beeps, use a quick pressure release. Open the lid.
5. Serve warm.

. . . .

GARLICKY LAMB LEG

Prep time: 35 minutes | Cook time: 50 minutes | Serves 6

INGREDIENTS:

* 910 g lamb leg
* 6 garlic cloves, minced
* 1 tsp. sea salt
* 1½ tsps. black pepper
* 2½ tbsps. olive oil
* 1½ small onions
* 360 ml bone stock
* 180 ml orange juice
* 6 sprigs thyme

DIRECTIONS:

1. In a bowl, whisk together the garlic, salt and pepper. Add the lamb leg to the bowl and marinate for 30 minutes.
2. Press the Sauté button on the Instant Pot and heat the olive oil. Add the onions and sauté for 4 minutes. Transfer the onions to a separate bowl.
3. Add the marinated lamb to the pot and sear for 3 minutes on each side, or lightly browned. Whisk in the cooked onions, stock, orange juice and thyme.
4. Close and secure the lid. Set the Instant Pot to the Meat/Stew mode and set the cooking time for 40 minutes on High Pressure. When the timer beeps, use a natural pressure release for 10 minutes, then release any remaining pressure. Carefully open the lid.
5. Divide the dish among 6 serving bowls and serve hot.

CHAPTER 8 SOUP AND STEW

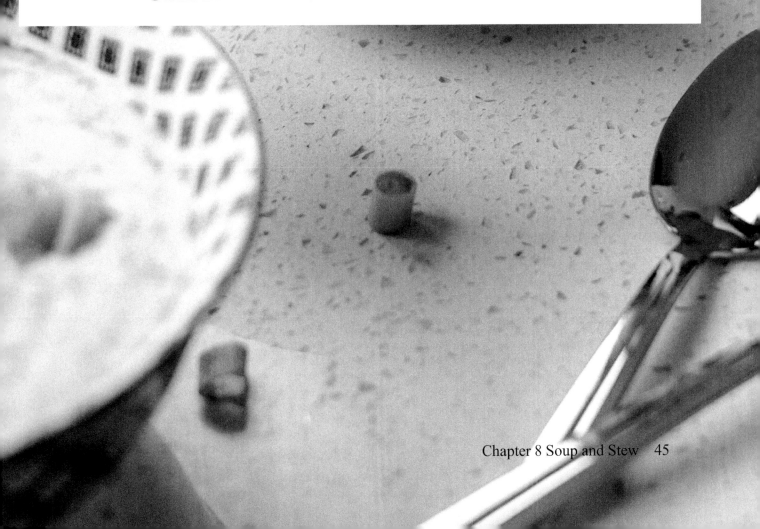

CHICKEN CHIPOTLE STEW

Prep time: 15 minutes | Cook time: 10 minutes | Serves 3

INGREDIENTS:

* 255 g chicken fillet, chopped
* 2 chipotle chili in adobo sauce, chopped
* 2 tbsps. sesame seeds
* 30 g fresh coriander, chopped
* 1 tsp. ground paprika
* ¼ tsp. salt
* 240 ml chicken stock

DIRECTIONS:

1. In a mixing bowl, combine the chicken fillet, chipotle chili, sesame seeds, coriander, ground paprika, and salt.
2. Transfer the mixture in the Instant Pot and pour in the chicken stock.
3. Select Manual mode and set cooking time for 10 minutes on High Pressure.
4. When timer beeps, use a natural pressure release for 10 minutes, then release any remaining pressure. Open the lid.
5. Serve warm.

. . . .

CALAMARI STEW

Prep time: 12 minutes | Cook time: 32 minutes | Serves 3

INGREDIENTS:

* 1 tbsp. olive oil
* 455 g separated calamari
* 60 ml white wine
* ½ bunch parsley, chopped
* 175 g tomatoes, chopped

DIRECTIONS:

1. Set the Instant Pot to Sauté and add the oil and calamari. Stir to combine well.
2. Lock the lid. Select the Manual mode, then set the timer for 9 minutes at Low Pressure.
3. Once the timer goes off, do a quick pressure release. Carefully open the lid.
4. Add the wine, tomatoes and half of the parsley, and stir well.
5. Lock the lid. Select the Manual mode, then set the timer for 25 minutes at High Pressure.
6. Once the timer goes off, do a quick pressure release. Carefully open the lid.
7. Sprinkle the remaining parsley on top. Divide the soup into bowls and serve.

. . . .

CABBAGE AND PORK SOUP

Prep time: 10 minutes | Cook time: 12 minutes | Serves 3

INGREDIENTS:

* 1 tsp. butter
* 35 g shredded white cabbage
* ½ tsp. ground coriander
* ½ tsp. salt
* ½ tsp. chili flakes
* 480 ml chicken stock
* 115 g pork mince

DIRECTIONS:

1. Melt the butter in the Instant Pot on Sauté mode.
2. Add cabbage and sprinkle with ground coriander, salt, and chili flakes.
3. Fold in the chicken stock and pork mince.
4. Close the lid and select Manual mode. Set cooking time for 12 minutes on High Pressure.
5. When timer beeps, use a quick pressure release. Open the lid.
6. Ladle the soup and serve warm.

CHICKEN CHILI VERDE SOUP

Prep time: 10 minutes | Cook time: 25 minutes | Serves 4

INGREDIENTS:

* 455 g chicken breast, skinless, boneless
* 1.2 L chicken stock
* 50 g Cheddar cheese, shredded
* 60 g chili Verde sauce
* 1 tbsp. dried coriander

DIRECTIONS:

1. Put chicken breast and chicken stock in the Instant Pot.
2. Add the coriander, Close the lid. Select Manual mode and set cooking time for 15 minutes on High Pressure.
3. When timer beeps, make a quick pressure release and open the lid.
4. Shred the chicken breast with a fork.
5. Add the Cheddar and chili Verde sauce in the soup and cook on Sauté mode for 10 minutes.
6. Mix in the dried coriander. Serve immediately.

ZOODLE AND CHICKEN SOUP

Prep time: 25 minutes | Cook time: 15 minutes | Serves 2

INGREDIENTS:

* 480 ml water
* 170 g chicken fillet, chopped
* 1 tsp. salt
* 60 g courgette, spiralized
* 1 tbsp. coconut aminos

DIRECTIONS:

1. Pour water in the Instant Pot. Add chopped chicken fillet and salt. Close the lid.
2. Select Manual mode and set cooking time for 15 minutes on High Pressure.
3. 1.When cooking is complete, perform a natural pressure release for 10 minutes, then release any remaining pressure. Open the lid.
4. 2.Fold in the zoodles and coconut aminos.
5. 3.Leave the soup for 10 minutes to rest. Serve warm.

PRAWNS AND CHICKEN THIGH STOCK

Prep time: 10 minutes | Cook time: 15 minutes | Serves 4

INGREDIENTS:

* 2 chicken thighs, boneless, chopped
* 115 g prawns, peeled
* 85 g sausages, chopped
* ½ pepper, chopped
* 240 ml beef stock
* 1 tsp. unsweetened tomato purée
* 1 celery stalk, chopped
* ½ tsp. Cajun seasonings

DIRECTIONS:

1. Heat the Instant Pot on Sauté mode for 3 minutes.
2. Add the chicken thighs, prawns, sausages, pepper, beef stock, unsweetened tomato purée, celery stalk, and Cajun seasonings.
3. Gently mix the ingredients and close the lid.
4. Select Manual mode and set time to 15 minutes on High Pressure.
5. When cooking is complete, use a quick pressure release and open the lid.
6. Serve immediately.

ORZO VEGGIE SOUP

Prep time: 15 minutes | Cook time: 10 minutes | Serves 4

INGREDIENTS:

* 1 medium potato, peeled and small-diced
* 1 medium courgette, diced
* 1 small carrot, peeled and diced
* 1 small yellow onion, peeled and diced
* 2 stalks celery, diced
* 1 (425-g) can diced tomatoes, undrained
* 2 cloves garlic, peeled and minced
* 80 g gluten-free orzo
* 1.2 L vegetable stock
* 2 tsps. dried oregano leaves
* 2 tsps. dried thyme leaves
* 1 tsp. salt
* 1 tsp. ground black pepper
* 90 g fresh baby spinach
* 4 tbsps. grated Parmesan cheese

DIRECTIONS:

1. Add all the ingredients, except for the spinach and Parmesan cheese, to the Instant Pot.
2. Lock the lid. Select the Manual setting and set the cooking time for 10 minutes at High Pressure. Once the timer goes off, use a quick pressure release. Carefully open the lid.
3. Stir in the spinach until wilted.
4. Ladle the soup into four bowls and garnish with the Parmesan cheese. Serve warm.

BEEF AND CHEESE SOUP

Prep time: 10 minutes | Cook time: 16 minutes | Serves 4

INGREDIENTS:

* 1 tbsp. olive oil
* 455 g beef mince
* 1 medium yellow onion, peeled and diced
* 1 small green pepper, deseeded and diced
* 1 medium carrot peeled and shredded
* 1 (425-g) can diced tomatoes, undrained
* 2 tsps. yellow mustard
* 1 tsp. garlic powder
* 1 tsp. smoked paprika
* ½ tsp. salt
* 960 ml beef stock
* 50 g shredded iceberg lettuce
* 100 g shredded Cheddar cheese, divided
* 80 g diced dill pickles

DIRECTIONS:

1. Set the Instant Pot to the Sauté mode and heat the olive oil for 30 seconds. Add the beef, onion and green pepper to the pot and sauté for 5 minutes, or until the beef is lightly browned. Add the carrot and sauté for 1 minute.
2. Stir in the tomatoes with juice, mustard, garlic powder, paprika, salt and beef stock.
3. Close and secure the lid. Select the Manual mode and set the cooking time for 7 minutes on High Pressure. When the timer goes off, use a quick pressure release. Carefully open the lid.
4. Whisk in the lettuce and 50 g of the cheese. Select the Sauté mode and cook for 3 minutes.
5. Divide the soup among 4 bowls and serve topped with the remaining cheese and dill pickles.

QUINOA AND CHICKEN STEW

Prep time: 30 minutes | Cook time: 23 minutes | Serves 6

INGREDIENTS:

* 570 g chicken thigh fillets
* 960 ml chicken stock
* 560 g chopped butternut squash
* 160 g chopped onion
* 90 g uncooked quinoa

DIRECTIONS:

1. Put the chicken in the Instant Pot. Add the chicken thigh fillets, stock, squash and chopped onion.
2. Lock the lid. Select the Manual mode, then set the timer for 8 minutes at High Pressure.
3. Once the timer goes off, do a quick pressure release. Carefully open the lid.
4. Stir the quinoa into the stew.
5. Set the Instant Pot to Sauté and cook for about 15 minutes, stirring occasionally.
6. Serve the stew in a large serving bowl.

CAULIFLOWER RICE AND CHICKEN THIGH SOUP

Prep time: 15 minutes | Cook time: 13 minutes | Serves 5

INGREDIENTS:

* 215 g cauliflower florets
* 455 g boneless, skinless chicken thighs
* 1.1 L chicken stock
* ½ yellow onion, chopped
* 2 garlic cloves, minced
* 1 tbsp. unflavored gelatin powder
* 2 tsps. sea salt
* ½ tsp. ground black pepper
* 55 g sliced courgette
* 40 g sliced turnips
* 1 tsp. dried parsley
* 3 celery stalks, chopped
* 1 tsp. ground turmeric
* ½ tsp. dried marjoram
* 1 tsp. dried thyme
* ½ tsp. dried oregano

DIRECTIONS:

1. Add the cauliflower florets to a food processor and pulse until a ricelike consistency is achieved. Set aside.
2. Add the chicken thighs, chicken stock, onions, garlic, gelatin powder, sea salt, and black pepper to the pot. Gently stir to combine.
3. Lock the lid. Select Manual mode and set cooking time for 10 minutes on High Pressure.
4. When cooking is complete, quick release the pressure and open the lid.
5. Transfer the chicken thighs to a cutting board. Chop the chicken into bite-sized pieces and then return the chopped chicken to the pot.
6. Add the cauliflower rice, courgette, turnips, parsley, celery, turmeric, marjoram, thyme, and oregano to the pot. Stir to combine.
7. Lock the lid. Select Manual mode and set cooking time for 3 minutes on High Pressure.
8. When cooking is complete, quick release the pressure.
9. Open the lid. Ladle the soup into serving bowls. Serve hot.

· ·

CHICKEN TOMATO STEW

Prep time: 12 minutes | Cook time: 30 minutes | Serves 8

INGREDIENTS:

* 4 onions, chopped
* 1 tbsp. olive oil
* 250 g chicken breast
* 150 g diced tomatoes
* 960 ml low-sodium chicken stock
* 60 ml water

DIRECTIONS:

1. Press the Sauté bottom on the Instant Pot.
2. Add and heat the olive oil.
3. Add the onions and sauté for 1 to 2 minutes until turn translucent and softened.
4. Add the chicken and evenly brown for 4 to 5 minutes.
5. Add the tomatoes and sauté for 2 minutes or until soft.
6. Pour in the stock and water.
7. Lock the lid. Press Manual. Set the timer to 20 minutes at High Pressure.
8. Once the timer goes off, press Cancel. Do a quick pressure release.
9. Open the lid, transfer them in a large bowl and serve.

CHICKEN SOUP WITH EGG NOODLES

Prep time: 15 minutes | Cook time: 24 minutes | Serves 8

INGREDIENTS:

*   1 (1.5-kg) chicken, cut into pieces
*   960 ml low-sodium chicken stock
*   3 stalks celery, chopped
*   2 medium carrots, peeled and chopped
*   1 medium yellow onion, peeled and chopped
*   1 clove garlic, and smashed
*   1 bay leaf
*   1 tsp. poultry seasoning
*   ½ tsp. dried thyme
*   1 tsp. salt
*   ¼ tsp. ground black pepper
*   115 g dried egg noodles

DIRECTIONS:

1. Add all the ingredients, except for the egg noodles, to the Instant Pot and stir to combine.
2. Set the lid in place. Select the Soup mode and set the cooking time for 20 minutes at High Pressure. Once cooking is complete, use a natural pressure release for 20 to 25 minutes, then release any remaining pressure. Carefully open the lid.
3. Remove and discard the bay leaf. Transfer the chicken to a clean work surface. Shred chicken and discard the skin and bones. Return the shredded chicken to the pot and stir to combine. Stir in the noodles.
4. Lock the lid. Select the Manual mode and set the cooking time for 4 minutes at High Pressure. Once cooking is complete, use a quick pressure release. Carefully open the lid.
5. Serve hot.

. . . .

CARROT AND CABBAGE BEEF STEW

Prep time: 10 minutes | Cook time: 19 minutes | Serves 4 to 6

INGREDIENTS:

*   3 tbsps. extra-virgin olive oil
*   2 large carrots, peeled and sliced into ½ cm disks and then quartered
*   1 large Spanish onion, diced
*   910 g beef mince
*   3 cloves garlic, minced
*   1 (1.3-kg) can tomato juice
*   480 ml vegetable stock
*   Juice of 2 lemons
*   1 head cabbage, cored and roughly chopped
*   100 g jasmine rice
*   60 g dark brown sugar
*   1 tbsp. Worcestershire sauce
*   2 tsps. seasoned salt
*   1 tsp. black pepper
*   3 bay leaves

DIRECTIONS:

1. Set the Instant Pot to the Sauté mode and heat the oil for 3 minutes. Add the carrots and onion to the pot and sauté for 3 minutes, or until just tender. Add the beef mince and garlic to the pot and sauté for 3 minutes, or until the beef is lightly browned. Stir in the remaining ingredients.
2. Lock the lid. Select the Manual mode and set the cooking time for 10 minutes on High Pressure. When the timer goes off, perform a quick pressure release. Carefully open the lid.
3. Let rest for 5 minutes to thicken and cool before serving.

CAULIFLOWER AND PROVOLONE SOUP

Prep time: 10 minutes | Cook time: 6 minutes | Serves 4

INGREDIENTS:

* 215 g chopped cauliflower
* 2 tbsps. fresh coriander
* 240 ml coconut cream
* 480 ml beef stock
* 85 g Provolone cheese, chopped

DIRECTIONS:

1. Put cauliflower, coriander, coconut cream, beef stock, and cheese in the Instant Pot. Stir to mix well.
2. Select Manual mode and set cooking time for 6 minutes on High Pressure.
3. When timer beeps, allow a natural pressure release for 4 minutes, then release any remaining pressure. Open the lid.
4. Blend the soup and ladle in bowls to serve.

. . . .

LAMB AND CHICKPEA SOUP

Prep time: 10 minutes | Cook time: 13 minutes | Serves 4

INGREDIENTS:

* 1 tbsp. olive oil
* 455 g lamb mince
* 1 medium red onion, peeled and diced
* 1 medium carrot, peeled and shredded
* 3 cloves garlic, peeled and minced
* 1 (425-g) can diced tomatoes, undrained
* 1 (440-g) can chickpeas, rinsed and drained
* 960 ml chicken stock
* ½ tsp. ground ginger
* ½ tsp. turmeric
* ½ tsp. salt
* ¼ tsp. ground cinnamon
* 20 g chopped fresh coriander
* 4 tbsps. plain full-fat Greek yogurt

DIRECTIONS:

1. Set the Instant Pot to the Sauté mode and heat the olive oil. Add the lamb and onion to the pot and sauté for 5 minutes, or until the lamb is lightly browned. Add the carrot and garlic to the pot and sauté for 1 minute.
2. Stir in the remaining ingredients, except for the coriander and Greek yogurt.
3. Set the lid in place. Select the Manual mode and set the cooking time for 7 minutes on High Pressure. When the timer goes off, perform a quick pressure release. Carefully open the lid.
4. Ladle the soup into 4 bowls and garnish with the coriander and yogurt. Serve warm.

CHAPTER 9 SNACK AND DESSERT

JALAPEÑO PEANUTS

Prep time: 3 hours 20 minutes | Cook time: 45 minutes | Serves 4

INGREDIENTS:

* 115 g raw peanuts in the shell
* 1 jalapeño, sliced
* 1 tbsp. Cajun seasoning
* ½ tbsp. cayenne pepper
* ½ tbsp. garlic powder
* 1 tbsp. salt

DIRECTIONS:

1. Add all ingredients to the Instant Pot. Pour in enough water to cover. Stir to mix well. Use a steamer to gently press down the peanuts.
2. Secure the lid. Choose the Manual mode and set the cooking time for 45 minutes at High pressure.
3. Once cooking is complete, perform a natural pressure release for 15 minutes, then release any remaining pressure. Carefully open the lid.
4. Transfer the peanut and the liquid in a bowl, then refrigerate for 3 hours before serving.

BACON WRAPPED SAUSAGES

Prep time: 15 minutes | Cook time: 3 minutes | Serves 10

INGREDIENTS:

* 455 g cocktail sausages
* 230 g bacon, cut into slices
* 2 tbsps. apple cider vinegar
* 60 g ketchup
* 1 tbsp. ground mustard
* 1 tbsp. onion powder
* 120 ml chicken stock
* Salt and ground black pepper, to taste
* 120 ml water

DIRECTIONS:

1. Wrap each cocktail wiener with a slice of bacon and secure with a toothpick.
2. Lay the bacon-wrapped cocktail sausages in the bottom of the Instant Pot. Repeat with the remaining cocktail sausages.
3. In a bowl, combine the remaining ingredients. Stir to mix well. Pour the mixture over the bacon-wrapped cocktail sausages.
4. Secure the lid. Choose the Manual mode and set the cooking time for 3 minutes on Low Pressure.
5. Once cooking is complete, perform a natural pressure release for 5 minutes, then release any remaining pressure. Carefully open the lid.
6. Serve immediately.

HERBED BUTTON MUSHROOMS

Prep time: 10 minutes | Cook time: 4 minutes | Serves 4

INGREDIENTS:

* 170 g button mushrooms, rinsed and drained
* 1 clove garlic, minced
* 120 ml vegetable stock
* ½ tsp. dried basil
* ½ tsp. onion powder
* ½ tsp. dried oregano
* ⅓ tsp. dried rosemary
* ½ tsp. smoked paprika
* Coarse sea salt and ground black pepper, to taste
* 1 tbsp. tomato paste
* 1 tbsp. butter

DIRECTIONS:

1. Put all the ingredients, except for the tomato paste and butter, in the Instant Pot. Stir to mix well.
2. Secure the lid. Choose the Manual mode and set the cooking time for 4 minutes at High pressure.
3. Once cooking is complete, perform a quick pressure release. Carefully open the lid.
4. Stir in the tomato paste and butter. Serve immediately.

BEEF PATTIES WITH LENTIL

Prep time: 25 minutes | Cook time: 25 minutes | Makes 15 patties

INGREDIENTS:

* 190 g dried yellow lentils
* 480 ml beef stock
* 230 g lean beef mince
* 40 g oats
* 2 large eggs, beaten
* 2 tsps. Sriracha sauce
* 2 tbsps. diced yellow onion
* ½ tsp. salt

DIRECTIONS:

1. Add the lentils and stock to the Instant Pot. Lock the lid.
2. Press the Manual button and set the cook time for 15 minutes on High Pressure. When the timer beeps, let pressure release naturally for 10 minutes, then release any remaining pressure. Unlock the lid.
3. Transfer the lentils to a medium bowl with a slotted spoon. Smash most of the lentils with the back of a spoon until chunky.
4. Add beef, oats, eggs, Sriracha, onion, and salt. Whisk to combine them well. Form the mixture into 15 patties.
5. Cook in a frying pan on stovetop over medium-high heat in batches for 10 minutes. Flip the patties halfway through.
6. Transfer patties to serving dish and serve warm.

. . . .

HUNGARIAN SQUARES

Prep time: 15 minutes | Cook time: 55 minutes | Serves 4

INGREDIENTS:

* 160 ml water, divided
* 160 g yellow polenta
* 240 g yogurt
* 1 egg, beaten
* 120 g sour cream
* 1 tsp. baking soda
* 2 tbsps. safflower oil
* ¼ tsp. salt
* 4 tbsps. plum jam

DIRECTIONS:

1. Pour 240 ml of water in the Instant Pot. Set a trivet in the pot. Spritz a baking pan with cooking spray.
2. Combine the polenta, yogurt, egg, sour cream, baking soda, 60 ml of water, safflower oil, and salt in a large bowl. Stir to mix well.
3. Pour the mixture into the prepared baking pan. Spread the plum jam over. Cover with aluminum foil. Lower the pan onto the trivet.
4. Secure the lid. Choose the Manual mode and set the cooking time for 55 minutes at High pressure. Once cooking is complete, perform a quick pressure release, carefully open the lid.
5. Transfer the polenta chunk onto a cooling rack and allow to cool for 10 minutes. Slice into squares and serve.

. . . .

HONEY RAISINS AND CARROTS

Prep time: 5 minutes | Cook time: 5 minutes | Serves 3

INGREDIENTS:

* 455 g carrots, peeled and cut into chunks
* 2 tbsps. golden raisins
* 120 ml water
* ½ tbsp. honey
* ⅔ tsp. crushed red pepper flakes
* ½ tbsp. melted butter
* Salt, to taste

DIRECTIONS:

1. Add the carrots, raisins, and water to the Instant Pot
2. Secure the lid and select the Manual function. Set the cooking time for 5 minutes on Low Pressure.
3. When the timer beeps, do a quick release, then open the lid.
4. Strain the carrots and transfer them to a large bowl.
5. Put the remaining ingredients into the bowl and toss well.
6. Serve warm.

POTATO CUBES

Prep time: 5 minutes | Cook time: 10 minutes | Serves 2

INGREDIENTS:

* 2½ medium potatoes, scrubbed and cubed
* 1 tbsp. chopped fresh rosemary
* ½ tbsp. olive oil
* Freshly ground black pepper, to taste
* 1 tbsp. fresh lemon juice
* 120 ml vegetable stock

DIRECTIONS:

1. Put the potatoes, rosemary, oil, and pepper to the Instant Pot. Stir to mix well.
2. Set to the Sauté mode and sauté for 4 minutes.
3. Fold in the remaining ingredients.
4. Secure the lid and select the Manual function. Set the cooking time for 6 minutes at High Pressure.
5. Once cooking is complete, do a quick release, then open the lid.
6. Serve warm.

. . . .

OAT AND BLACK BEAN BROWNIES

Prep time: 5 minutes | Cook time: 25 minutes | Serves 4

INGREDIENTS:

* 360 g canned black beans, drained
* 40 g oats
* ½ tsp. salt
* 3 tbsps. unsweetened cocoa powder
* 160 g maple syrup
* 60 ml coconut oil
* ¾ tsp. baking powder
* 85 g chocolate chips
* Cooking spray
* 360 ml water

DIRECTIONS:

1. Pulse the black beans, oats, salt, cocoa powder, maple syrup, coconut oil, and baking powder in a food processor until very smooth.
2. Pour the batter into a medium bowl and fold in the chocolate chips.
3. Spray a 18 cm springform pan with cooking spray and pour in the batter. Cover the pan with aluminum foil.
4. Pour the water into the Instant Pot and insert a trivet. Place the pan on the trivet.
5. Lock the lid. Select the Manual mode and set the cooking time for 25 minutes at High Pressure.
6. When the timer beeps, perform a natural pressure release for 10 minutes, then release any remaining pressure. Carefully remove the lid.
7. Let cool for 5 minutes, then transfer to the fridge to chill for 1 to 2 hours.
8. Cut the brownies into squares and serve.

. . . .

COCONUT BROWN RICE PUDDING

Prep time: 15 minutes | Cook time: 22 minutes | Serves 6

INGREDIENTS:

* 200 g long-grain brown rice, rinsed
* 480 ml water
* 1 (425-g) can full-fat coconut milk
* ½ tsp. pure vanilla extract
* ½ tsp. ground cinnamon
* 105 g maple syrup
* Pinch fine sea salt

DIRECTIONS:

1. Combine the rice and water in the Instant Pot and secure the lid. Select the Manual mode and set the cooking time for 22 minutes on Low Pressure.
2. When timer beeps, allow the pressure to naturally release for 10 minutes, then release any remaining pressure. Carefully open the lid.
3. Add the coconut milk, vanilla, cinnamon, maple syrup, and salt. Stir well to combine.
4. Use an immersion blender to pulse the pudding until creamy. Serve warm or you can refrigerate the pudding for an hour before serving.

BULLETPROOF HOT CHOCO

Prep time: 6 minutes | Cook time: 5 minutes | Serves 1

INGREDIENTS:

* 2 tbsps. coconut oil, divided
* 120 ml coconut milk
* 120 ml water
* 2 tbsps. unsweetened cocoa powder
* Dash of cinnamon
* 1 tsp. erythritol

DIRECTIONS:

1. Place 1 tbsp. of coconut oil and milk in the Instant Pot and pour in the water.
2. Lock the lid. Set the Instant Pot to Manual mode, then set the timer for 5 minutes at High Pressure.
3. When the timer goes off, perform a quick release.
4. Open the lid and press the Sauté button.
5. Add 1 tbsp. of coconut oil, cocoa powder, cinnamon and erythritol. Stir to combine well and the mixture has a thick consistency.
6. Transfer the mixture on a baking sheet, then put the sheet in the refrigerator for several hours. Serve chilled.

. . . .

BEER POACHED PEARS

Prep time: 5 minutes | Cook time: 10 minutes | Serves 2

INGREDIENTS:

* 3 peeled (stem on) firm pears
* 1 bottle stout beer
* 105 g packed brown sugar
* 1 vanilla bean, split lengthwise and seeds scraped

DIRECTIONS:

1. Slice a thin layer from the bottom of each pear so they can stand upright. Use a melon baller to scoop out the seeds and core from the bottom.
2. Stir together the beer, brown sugar, and vanilla bean and seeds in the Instant Pot until combined. Place the pears upright in the pot.
3. Lock the lid. Select the Manual mode and set the cooking time for 9 minutes at High Pressure.
4. When the timer beeps, perform a quick pressure release. Carefully remove the lid.
5. Using tongs, carefully remove the pears by their stems and transfer to a plate and set aside.
6. Set the Instant Pot to Sauté and simmer until the liquid in the Instant Pot is reduced by half.
7. Strain the liquid into a bowl through a fine-mesh sieve, then pour over the pears.
8. Serve at room temperature or chilled.

. . . .

CARAMEL APPLE COBBLER

Prep time: 30 minutes | Cook time: 2 minutes | Serves 4

INGREDIENTS:

* 5 apples, cored, peeled, and cut into 2.5 cm cubes, at room temperature
* 2 tbsps. caramel syrup
* ½ tsp. ground nutmeg
* 2 tsps. ground cinnamon
* 2 tbsps. maple syrup
* 120 ml water
* 60 g oats
* 30 g plain flour
* 70 g brown sugar
* 4 tbsps. salted butter, softened
* ½ tsp. sea salt
* Vanilla ice cream, for serving

DIRECTIONS:

1. Place the apples in the Instant Pot and top with the caramel syrup, nutmeg, cinnamon, maple syrup, and water. Stir to coat well.
2. Combine the oats, flour, brown sugar, butter and salt in a large bowl. Mix well and pour over the apple mixture in the pot.
3. Secure the lid, then select the Manual mode and set the cooking time for 2 minutes on High Pressure.
4. When cooking is complete, perform a natural pressure release for 20minutes, then release any remaining pressure. Carefully open the lid.
5. Transfer the cobbler to a plate, then topped with vanilla ice cream and serve.

BOURBON AND DATE PUDDING CAKE

Prep time: 15 minutes | Cook time: 25 minutes | Serves 4

INGREDIENTS:

* 80 g plain flour
* ¼ tsp. allspice
* ½ tsp. baking soda
* ¼ tsp. cloves powder
* ½ tsp. cinnamon powder
* ¼ tsp. salt
* 1 tsp. baking powder
* 2 tbsps. bourbon
* 3 tbsps. unsalted butter, melted
* 6 tbsps. hot water
* 2 tbsps. whole milk
* 1 egg, beaten
* 75 g chopped dates
* 240 ml water
* 120 g caramel sauce

DIRECTIONS:

1. In a bowl, combine the flour, allspice, baking soda, cloves, cinnamon, salt, and baking powder.
2. In another bowl, mix the bourbon, butter, hot water, and milk. Pour the bourbon mixture into the flour mixture and mix until well mixed. Whisk in egg and fold in dates.
3. Spritz 4 medium ramekins with cooking spray. Divide the mixture among them, and cover with foil.
4. Pour the water in the Instant Pot, then fit in a trivet and place ramekins on top.
5. Seal the lid, select the Manual mode and set the cooking time for 25 minutes at High Pressure.
6. When cooking is complete, perform a natural pressure release for 10 minutes, then release any remaining pressure.
7. Unlock the lid and carefully remove ramekins, invert onto plates, and drizzle caramel sauce on top. Serve warm.

APPLE BREAD

Prep time: 12 minutes | Cook time: 1 hour | Serves 4

INGREDIENTS:

* 1 tbsp. baking powder
* 3 eggs
* 360 ml sweetened condensed milk
* 300 g white flour
* 3 apples, peeled, cored and chopped
* 1 tbsp. melted coconut oil
* 240 ml water

DIRECTIONS:

1. In a bowl, mix the baking powder with eggs and whisk well.
2. Add the milk, flour and apple pieces, whisk well and pour into a loaf pan greased with coconut oil.
3. In the Instant Pot, add the water. Arrange a trivet in the pot, then place the loaf pan on the trivet.
4. Lock the lid. Set the Instant Pot to Slow Cook mode, then set the timer for 1 hour at High Pressure.
5. When the timer goes off, perform a natural release for 10 minutes, then release any remaining pressure. Carefully open the lid.
6. Leave apple bread to cool down, slice and serve.

APRICOTS DULCE DE LECHE

Prep time: 15 minutes | Cook time: 25 minutes | Serves 6

INGREDIENTS:

* 1.2 L water
* 480 g sweetened condensed milk
* 4 apricots, halved, cored, and sliced

DIRECTIONS:

1. Pour the water in the Instant Pot and fit in a trivet. Divide condensed milk into 6 medium jars and close with lids. Place jars on trivet.
2. Seal the lid, set to the Manual mode and set the timer for 25 minutes at High Pressure.
3. When cooking is complete, use a natural pressure release for 10 minutes, then release any remaining pressure. Unlock the lid.
4. Use a fork to whisk until creamy. Serve with sliced apricots.

APPENDIX 1: MEASUREMENT CONVERSION CHART

WEIGHT EQUIVALENTS

METRIC	US STANDARD	US STANDARD (OUNCES)
15 g	1 tablespoon	1/2 ounce
30 g	1/8 cup	1 ounce
60 g	1/4 cup	2 ounces
115 g	1/2 cup	4 ounces
170 g	3/4 cup	6 ounces
225 g	1 cup	8 ounces
450 g	2 cups	16 ounces
900 g	4 cups	2 pounds

VOLUME EQUIVALENTS

METRIC	US STANDARD	US STANDARD (OUNCES)
15 ml	1 tablespoon	1/2 fl.oz.
30 ml	2 tablespoons	1 fl.oz.
60 ml	1/4 cup	2 fl.oz.
125 ml	1/2 cup	4 fl.oz.
180 ml	3/4 cup	6 fl.oz.
250 ml	1 cup	8 fl.oz.
500 ml	2 cups	16 fl.oz.
1000 ml	4 cups	1 quart

TEMPERATURES EQUIVALENTS

CELSIUS (C)	FAHRENHEIT (F) (APPROXIMATE)
120 °C	250 °F
135 °C	275 °F
150 °C	300 °F
160 °C	325 °F
175 °C	350 °F
190 °C	375 °F
205 °C	400 °F
220 °C	425 °F
230 °C	450 °F
245°C	475 °F
260 °C	500 °F

LENGTH EQUIVALENTS

METRIC	IMPERIAL
3 mm	1/8 inch
6 mm	1/4 inch
1 cm	1/2 inch
2.5 cm	1 inch
3 cm	1 1/4 inches
5 cm	2 inches
10 cm	4 inches
15 cm	6 inches
20 cm	8 inches

APPENDIX 2: 365 DAYS MEAL PLAN

Day 1-5	Raisin and Apple Oatmeal	Feta and Red Onion Couscous Pilaf	Mustard Macaroni and Cheese	Bruschetta Chicken	Pork with Brussels Sprouts
Day 6-10	Indian Butter Chicken	Spinach and Pine Nut Fusilli Pasta	Vanilla Pancake	Chicken Chipotle Stew	Jalapeño Peanuts
Day 11-15	Grape Leaves and Nut Rice Bowl	Buckwheat and Strawberry Pudding	Calamari Stew	Greek Lamb Loaf	Hungarian Squares
Day 16-20	Greek Lamb Leg	Lemon Garlic Chicken	Bacon Wrapped Sausages	Cherry Tomato Farfalle with Pesto	Chicken Chili Verde Soup
Day 21-25	Garlicky Baby Bok Choy	Herbed Button Mushrooms	Mongolian Chicken	Apple Bread	Veggie Stew
Day 26-30	Spinach and Mushroom Pasta	Cabbage and Pork Soup	Garlicky Baby Potatoes	Beef Patties with Lentil	Apricots Dulce de Leche
Day 31-35	Zoodle and Chicken Soup	WOrange Chicken Breasts	Potato Cubes	Prawns and Broccoli Quinoa Bowl	Italian Carrot and Potato Medley
Day 36-40	Pork with Peppers	Spinach Lemon Pasta	Oat and Black Bean Brownies	Jamaican Curry Chicken Drumsticks	Honey Raisins and Carrots
Day 41-45	Beef Mince Pasta	Bourbon and Date Pudding Cake	Lamb Burgers	Mushroom Polenta	Peanut Butter Granola Bars
Day 40-50	Prawns and Chicken Thigh Stock	Artichokes with Onion	Harissa Lamb	Coconut Brown Rice Pudding	Pork with Mushroom Sauce
Day 51-55	Cranberry and Almond Quinoa Pilaf	Orzo Veggie Soup	Green Beans with Coconut	Garlicky Lamb Leg	Bulletproof Hot Choco
Day 56-60	Caramel Apple Cobbler	Asparagus and Gruyère Cheese Frittata	Instant Pot Ranch Chicken	Beef and Cheese Soup	Broccoli with Roasted Almonds
Day 61-65	Chicken Enchilada Bowl	Cranberry and Almond Quinoa Pilaf	Quinoa and Chicken Stew	Caper and Olive Pasta	Beer Poached Pears
Day 66-70	Pasta Carbonara	Pearl Barley with Peppers	Paprika Chicken with Tomatoes	Caper and Olive Pasta	Cauliflower Rice and Chicken Thigh Soup
Day 71-75	Egg Benedict	Spinach and Tomato Couscous	Chicken Tomato Stew	Courgette Sticks	Jalapeño Peanuts
Day 76-80	Mushrooms with Garlic	Quinoa and Chicken Stew	Quinoa Risotto	Indian Butter Chicken	Caramel Apple Cobbler
Day 81-85	Penne Pasta with Tomato-Vodka Sauce	Honey-Glazed Chicken with Sesame	Honey Raisins and Carrots	Bacon and Egg Risotto	Pork with Brussels Sprouts
Day 86-90	Bow Tie Past	Farro Risotto with Mushroom	Mexican Shredded Chicken	Apple Bread	Chicken Soup with Egg Noodles

Day 91-95	Mexican Beef Shred	Instant Pot Ranch Chicken	Cauliflower and Provolone Soup	Seafood Pasta with Tomatoes	Beef and Cheese Soup
Day 96-100	Pork Chops with Onions	Spinach and Ham Frittata	Bourbon and Date Pudding Cake	Carrot and Cabbage Beef Stew	Jamaican Curry Chicken Drumsticks
Day 101-105	Apricots Dulce de Leche	Mushroom Barley Risotto	Steamed Asparagus	Grape Leaves and Nut Rice Bowl	Huli Huli Chicken
Day 106-110	Lemon Beef Meal	Jalapeño Peanuts	Garlicky Baby Bok Choy	Coffee Cake	Greek Lamb Loaf
Day 111-115	Courgette Penne Pasta	Spicy Chicken Bulgur	Lemony Chicken with Potatoes	Veggie Stew	Greek Lamb Leg
Day 116-120	Cabbage and Pork Soup	French Eggs	Prawns and Broccoli Quinoa Bowl	Mexican Shredded Chicken	Courgette Sticks
Day 121-125	Cauliflower Tots	Beef Mince Pasta	Pork Chops with Sauerkraut	Mushrooms with Garlic	Eggs En Cocotte
Day 126-130	Bulletproof Hot Choco	Prawns and Broccoli Quinoa Bowl	French Eggs	Lamb and Chickpea Soup	Steamed Asparagus
Day 131-135	Quinoa with Spinach	Broccoli with Roasted Almonds	Cranberry and Almond Quinoa Pilaf	Ratatouille	Coconut Brown Rice Pudding
Day 136-140	Beer Poached Pears	Mongolian Glazed Beef	Italian Carrot and Potato Medley	Lemony Chicken with Potatoes	Penne Pasta with Tomato-Vodka Sauce
Day 141-145	Lemony Fennel Chicken	Quinoa and Tomato Cream Bowl	Pork with Brussels Sprouts	Korean Beef Ribs	Lemongrass Rice and Beef Pot
Day 146-150	Duo-Cheese Mushroom Pasta	Mushroom Barley Risotto	Coffee Cake	Gobi Masala	Carrot and Cabbage Beef Stew
Day 151-155	Indian Butter Chicken	Korean Beef Ribs	Green Beans with Coconut	Spicy Chicken Bulgur	Beef and Cheese Soup
Day 156-160	Raisin and Cranberry Compote	Kale Chicken Soup	Farro Risotto with Mushroom	Gobi Masala	Quinoa and Chicken Stew
Day 161-165	Penne Pasta with Tomato-Vodka Sauce	Tuna Noodle Casserole with Cheese	Lemon Garlic Chicken	Black-eyed Bean Rice Bowl	Ratatouille
Day 166-170	Mushroom Polenta	Spinach Lemon Pasta	Artichoke Corn Risotto	Vegetable Burgers	Vegetable Burgers
Day 171-175	Pearl Barley with Peppers	Mustard Macaroni and Cheese	Mongolian Glazed Beef	Parmesan Risotto	Pork with Mushroom Sauce
Day 176-180	Instant Pot Ranch Chicken	Chicken Tomato Stew	Quinoa and Tomato Cream Bowl	Harissa Lamb	Spinach and Mushroom Pasta
Day 181-185	Feta and Red Onion Couscous Pilaf	Chicken Enchilada Bowl	Beef Mince Pasta	Caramel Apple Cobbler	Raisin and Apple Oatmeal
Day 186-190	Orange Chicken Breasts	Black-eyed Bean Rice Bowl	Oat and Black Bean Brownies	Caper and Olive Pasta	Greek Lamb Leg

Day 191-195	Eggs In Purgatory	Cauliflower Rice and Chicken Thigh Soup	Grape Leaves and Nut Rice Bowl	Quinoa Risotto	Jamaican Curry Chicken Drumsticks
Day 196-200	Pasta Carbonara	Spinach and Ham Frittata	Mexican Shredded Chicken	Mint and Pea Risotto	Bourbon and Date Pudding Cake
Day 201-205	Quinoa with Spinach	Lemony Fennel Chicken	Tuna Noodle Casserole with Cheese	Bulletproof Hot Choco	Artichoke Corn Risotto
Day 206-210	Artichokes with Onion	Farro Risotto with Mushroom	Feta and Rocket Pasta Salad	Korean Beef Ribs	Huli Huli Chicken
Day 211-215	Pearl Barley with Peppers	Courgette Sticks	Spinach and Tomato Couscous	Lemony Chicken with Potatoes	Chicken Soup with Egg Noodles
Day 216-220	Parmesan Risotto	Lemongrass Rice and Beef Pot	Lamb and Chickpea Soup	Spinach and Tomato Couscous	Beef Patties with Lentil
Day 221-225	Hungarian Squares	Mint and Pea Risotto	Garlicky Lamb Leg	Cabbage and Pork Soup	Garlicky Baby Potatoes
Day 226-230	Greek Lamb Loaf	Chicken Tomato Stew	Mint and Pea Risotto	Potato Cubes	Peanut Butter Granola Bars
Day 231-235	Mustard Macaroni and Cheese	Chicken Chili Verde Soup	Vanilla Pancake	Instant Pot Ranch Chicken	Mexican Beef Shred
Day 236-240	Carrot and Cabbage Beef Stew	Spinach Lemon Pasta	Pork with Peppers	Beer Poached Pears	Hawaiian Sweet Potato Hash
Day 241-245	Buckwheat and Strawberry Pudding	Pork with Mushroom Sauce	Garlicky Baby Bok Choy	Pasta Carbonara	Chicken Enchilada Bowl
Day 246-250	Parmesan Risotto	Zoodle and Chicken Soup	French Eggs	Broccoli with Roasted Almonds	Courgette Penne Pasta
Day 251-255	Spinach and Pine Nut Fusilli Pasta	Mongolian Chicken	Harissa Lamb	Quinoa and Tomato Cream Bowl	Green Beans with Coconut
Day 256-260	Steamed Asparagus	Mushroom Barley Risotto	Tuna Noodle Casserole with Cheese	Kale Chicken Soup	Cherry Tomato Farfalle with Pesto
Day 261-265	Orange Chicken Breasts	Duo-Cheese Mushroom Pasta	Cauliflower Tots	Spinach and Ham Frittata	Orzo Veggie Soup
Day 266-270	Huli Huli Chicken	Herbed Button Mushrooms	Eggs In Purgatory	Garlicky Baby Bok Choy	Spinach and Mushroom Pasta
Day 271-275	Eggs En Cocotte	Bow Tie Pasta	Steamed Asparagus	Black-eyed Bean Rice Bowl	Mongolian Glazed Beef
Day 276-280	Pork Chops with Sauerkraut	Asparagus and Gruyère Cheese Frittata	Lemon Beef Meal	Lemon Garlic Chicken	Italian Carrot and Potato Medley
Day 281-285	Lamb Burgers	Bruschetta Chicken	Mushrooms with Garlic	Bacon and Egg Risotto	Calamari Stew
Day 286-290	Spicy Chicken Bulgur	Chicken Soup with Egg Noodles	Pork Chops with Onions	Apple Bread	Peanut Butter Granola Bars

Day 291-295	Egg Benedict	Chicken Chili Verde Soup	Paprika Chicken with Tomatoes	Pork with Brussels Sprouts	Quinoa Risotto
Day 296-300	Seafood Pasta with Tomatoes	Lemony Fennel Chicken	Mongolian Glazed Beef	Buckwheat and Strawberry Pudding	Garlicky Lamb Leg
Day 301-305	Cauliflower and Provolone Soup	Coffee Cake	Lemongrass Rice and Beef Pot	Pasta Carbonara	Honey-Glazed Chicken with Sesame
Day 306-310	Mexican Beef Shred	Chicken Chipotle Stew	Raisin and Apple Oatmeal	Cauliflower Tots	Lamb Burgers
Day 311-315	Artichoke Corn Risotto	Bacon Wrapped Sausages	Feta and Rocket Pasta Salad	Ratatouille	Courgette Penne Pasta
Day 316-320	Honey Raisins and Carrots	Pork Chops with Onions	Prawns and Chicken Thigh Stock	Feta and Red Onion Couscous Pilaf	Lemongrass Rice and Beef Pot
Day 321-325	Kale Chicken Soup	Beef Patties with Lentil	Quinoa with Spinach	Gobi Masala	Lamb and Chickpea Soup
Day 326-330	Vanilla Pancake	Hungarian Squares	Cauliflower Rice and Chicken Thigh Soup	Mongolian Chicken	Vegetable Burgers
Day 331-335	Pork Chops with Sauerkraut	Artichokes with Onion	Eggs En Cocotte	Cauliflower and Provolone Soup	Cherry Tomato Farfalle with Pesto
Day 336-340	Orzo Veggie Soup	Hawaiian Sweet Potato Hash	Cauliflower Tots	Paprika Chicken with Tomatoes	Herbed Button Mushrooms
Day 341-345	Spinach and Pine Nut Fusilli Pasta	Zoodle and Chicken Soup	Oat and Black Bean Brownies	Raisin and Cranberry Compote	Garlicky Baby Potatoes
Day 346-350	Veggie Stew	Duo-Cheese Mushroom Pasta	Calamari Stew	Potato Cubes	Feta and Rocket Pasta Salad
Day 351-355	Honey-Glazed Chicken with Sesame	Apricots Dulce de Leche	Seafood Pasta with Tomatoes	Chicken Tomato Stew	Egg Benedict
Day 356-360	Chicken Chipotle Stew	Asparagus and Gruyère Cheese Frittata	Coconut Brown Rice Pudding	Prawns and Chicken Thigh Stock	Orange Chicken Breasts
Day 361-365	Bow Tie Pasta	Lemon Beef Meal	Bruschetta Chicken	Bacon and Egg Risotto	Pork with Peppers

APPENDIX 3: INSTANT POT COOKING TIMETABLE

Poultry			
Items	**Minutes Under Pressure**	**Pressure**	**Release**
Chicken breast, bone-in	8 (steamed)	Low	Natural 5 mins, then Quick
Chicken breast, boneless	5 (steamed)	Low	Natural 8 mins, then Quick
Chicken thigh, bone-in	12 to 15	High	Natural 10 mins, then Quick
Chicken thigh, boneless, whole	8	High	Natural 10 mins, then Quick
Chicken thigh, 2-4-cm pieces	5 to 6	High	Quick
Chicken, whole (seared on all sides)	14 to 18	Low	Natural 8 mins, then Quick
Duck quarters, bone-in	35	High	Quick
Turkey breast, tenderloin (350 g)	5 (steamed)	Low	Natural 8 mins, then Quick
Turkey thigh, bone-in	30	High	Natural

Meat			
Items	**Minutes Under Pressure**	**Pressure**	**Release**
Beef, shoulder (chuck) roast (900 g)	35 to 45	High	Natural
Beef, shoulder (chuck), 4-cm chunks	20	High	Natural 10 mins, then Quick
Beef, bone-in short ribs	40	High	Natural
Beef, flat-iron steak, cut into 1-cm strips	6	Low	Quick
Beef, sirloin steak, cut into 1-cm strips	3	Low	Quick
Lamb, shanks	40	High	Natural
Lamb, shoulder, 4-cm	35	High	Natural
Pork back ribs (steamed)	25	High	Quick
Pork spare ribs (steamed)	20	High	Quick
Pork shoulder roast (900 g)	25	High	Natural
Pork, shoulder, 4-cm chunks	20	High	Quick
Pork tenderloin	4	Low	Quick
Smoked pork sausage, 1-cm slices	5 to 10	High	Quick

Beans and Legumes			
Items	**Minutes Under Pressure**	**Pressure**	**Release**
Black beans	8 or 9	Low or High	Natural
Black-eyed beans	5	High	Natural 8 mins, then Quick
Butter beans	4 or 5	Low or High	Natural 5 mins, then Quick
Cannellini beans	5 or 7	Low or High	Natural
Chickpeas	4	High	Natural 3 mins, then Quick
Kidney beans	5 or 7	Low or High	Natural
Lentils, brown (unsoaked)	20	High	Natural 10 mins, then Quick
Lentils, red (unsoaked)	10	High	Natural 5 mins, then Quick
Pinto beans	8 or 10	Low or High	Natural
Soybeans, dried	12 or 14	Low or High	Natural
Soybeans, fresh (edamame), unsoaked	1	High	Quick
Split peas (unsoaked)	5 to 8	Low or High	Natural

*For any foods labeled Natural release, allow at least 15 minutes natural pressure release before releasing remaining pressure.

Fish and Seafood

Items	Minutes Under Pressure	Pressure	Release
Clams	2	High	Quick
Halibut (2-cm thick)	3	High	Quick
Mussels	1	High	Quick
Prawn (frozen)	1	Low	Quick
Salmon (2-cm thick)	5	Low	Quick
Tilapia or cod (frozen)	3	Low	Quick

Grain and Rice

Items	Liquid per 220 g Grain	Minutes Under Pressure	Pressure	Release
Arborio (or other medium-grain) rice	375 ml	6 to 20 (depending on use)	High	Quick
Barley, pearled	625 ml	20	High	Natural 10 mins, then Quick
Brown rice, long grain	375 ml	13	High	Natural 10 mins, then Quick
Brown rice, medium-grain	375 ml	6 to 8	High	Natural
Buckwheat	450 ml	3 to 4	High	Natural
Oats, rolled	750 ml	3 to 4	High	Quick
Coarse oatmeal	1 L	12	High	Natural
Farro, pearled	500 ml	6 to 8	High	Natural
Farro, whole-grain	750 ml	22 to 24	High	Natural
Quinoa	375 ml	1	High	Natural 12 mins, then Quick
Wheat berries	375 ml	30	High	Natural 10 mins, then Quick
Long-grain white rice	250 ml	3	High	Natural
Wild rice	300 ml	22 to 24	High	Natural

Vegetables

Items	Prep	Minutes Under Pressure	Pressure	Release
Artichokes, large	Whole	15	High	Quick
Beetroots	Quartered if large; halved if small	9	High	Natural
Broccoli	Cut into florets	1	Low	Quick
Brussels sprouts	Halved	2	High	Quick
Butternut squash	Peeled, cut into 1-cm chunks	8	High	Quick
Cabbage	Sliced	5	High	Quick
Carrots	1-2-cm slices	2	High	Quick
Cauliflower	Whole	6	High	Quick
Cauliflower	Cut into florets	1	Low	Quick
Courgette	Peeled, cut into 1-cm chunks	7	High	Quick
Green beans	Cut in half or thirds	1	Low	Quick
Potatoes, large russet	Quartered; for mashing	8	High	Natural 8 mins, then Quick
Potatoes, red	Whole if less than 4-cm across, halved if larger	4	High	Quick
Spaghetti marrow	Halved lengthwise	7	High	Quick
Sweet potatoes	Halved lengthwise	8	High	Natural

APPENDIX 4: RECIPES INDEX

Printed in Great Britain
by Amazon

25674087R00044